787.87 GUITAR 5-03 ✓

Guitar TAB 2001-2002.

RECORDED VERSIONS
GUITAR

AUTHENTIC TRANSCRIPTIONS
WITH NOTES AND TABLATURE

GUITAR **TAB** 2001 2002

14.95

D0897312

CONTENTS

ISBN 0-634-04508-3

HAL•LEONARD®
CORPORATION

7777 W. BLUEMOUND RD. P.O. BOX 13819 MILWAUKEE, WI 53213

For all works contained herein:
Unauthorized copying, arranging, adapting, recording or public performance is an infringement of copyright.
Infringers are liable under the law.

CHARLES CITY PUBLIC LIBRARY
106 Milwaukee Mall
Charles City, IA 50616-2281

Visit Hal Leonard Online at
www.halleonard.com

Alive

Words and Music by Sonny, Marcos, Traa and Wuv

Copyright © 2001 by Famous Music Corporation and Souljah Music
All Rights Administered by Famous Music Corporation
International Copyright Secured All Rights Reserved

Androgyny

Words and Music by Duke Erikson, Shirley Ann Manson, Steve Marker and Butch Vig

* Synth. arr. for gtr.   ** Chord symbols reflect overall harmony.

Copyright © 2001 IRVING MUSIC, INC., VIBECRUSHER MUSIC, ALMO MUSIC CORP. and DEADARM MUSIC
All Rights for VIBECRUSHER MUSIC Controlled and Administered by IRVING MUSIC, INC.
All Rights for DEADARM MUSIC Controlled and Administered by ALMO MUSIC CORP.
All Rights Reserved   Used by Permission

Chorus

Outro

Chop Suey!

Words and Music by Daron Malakian and Serj Tankian

Copyright © 2001 Sony/ATV Tunes LLC and Ddevil Music
All Rights Administered by Sony/ATV Music Publishing, 8 Music Square West, Nashville, TN 37203
International Copyright Secured   All Rights Reserved

* Chord symbols reflect implied harmony.

Verse

1., 2. Wake up, grab a brush and put a lit - tle make-up. Hide the scars to fade a - way the
Whispered: (Wake up.

Gtr. 4: w/ Rhy. Fig. 3 (3 times)

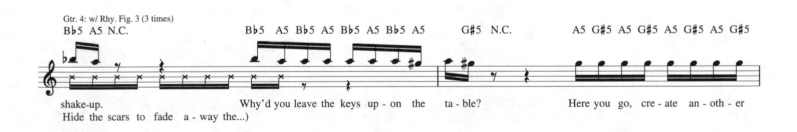

shake-up. Why'd you leave the keys up - on the ta - ble? Here you go, cre - ate an - oth - er
Hide the scars to fade a - way the...)

fa - ble, you want - ed to. Grab a brush and put a lit - tle make-up, you want - ed to. Hide the scars to fade a - way the

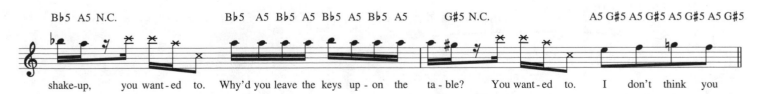

shake-up, you want - ed to. Why'd you leave the keys up - on the ta - ble? You want - ed to. I don't think you

Chorus
Half-time feel

trust   in   my   self - right-eous su - i -

End half-time feel
(1st time only)

cide. __   I   cry __   when an - gels de - serve to __

1.

Interlude
Gtrs. 2 & 4: w/ Rhy. Fig. 2 (2 times)

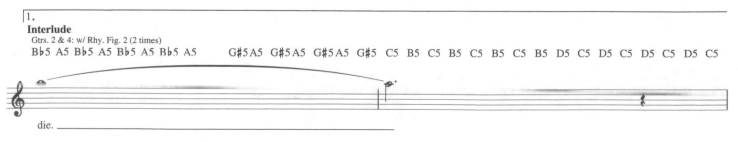

die. _____

14

Gtrs. 2 & 4: w/ Rhy. Figs. 4 & 4A (4 3/4 times)
Gtr. 3: w/ Riff D

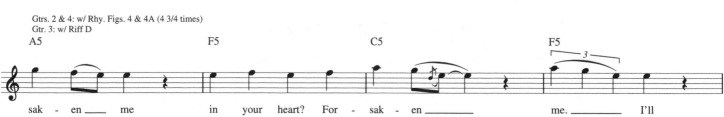

sak - en ___ me   in   your   heart? For - sak - en _____ me. _____ I'll

trust   in _____ my _____ self - right - eous su - i - cide. _____

I _____ cry _____ when an - gels de - serve to die _____ in _____

my _____ self - right - eous su - i - cide. _____ I _____ cry _____ when

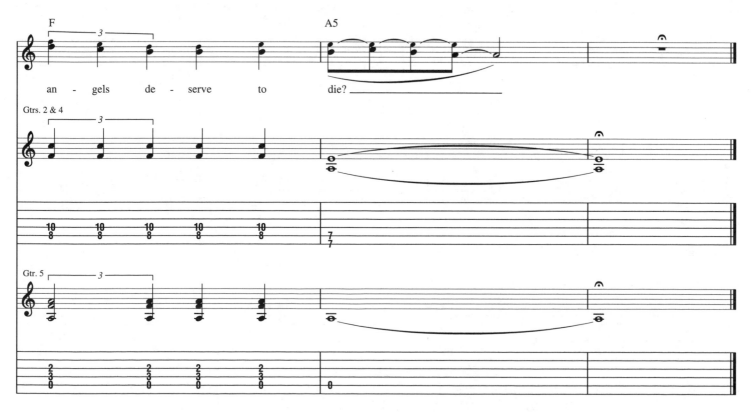

an - gels de - serve to die? _____

Gtrs. 2 & 4

Gtr. 5

Click Click Boom

Words and Music by Josey Scott, Chris Dabaldo, Wayne Swinney, Dave Novotny, Paul Crosby and Bob Marlette

Copyright © 2001 ALMO MUSIC CORP., FIVE SUPERSTARS, UNIVERSAL MUSIC CORP. and BLACK LAVA PRODUCTIONS
All Rights for FIVE SUPERSTARS Administered by ALMO MUSIC CORP.
All Rights for BLACK LAVA PRODUCTIONS Administered by UNIVERSAL MUSIC CORP.
All Rights Reserved   Used by Permission

Verse

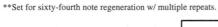

Gtr. 2 tacet
2nd time, Gtr. 5: w/ Fill 1 (4 times)

Sat - ur - days _ when kids go out and play, _ yo, I was up in my room, _ I let the ster - e - o blaze. Was - n't
2. What the hell _ is wrong with me? My mom and dad were - n't per - fect, but still you don't

Gtr. 3 (dist.) **Riff A** — **End Riff A**

mf
Harm. — — — — — ¬
w/ ring modulator

Gtr. 1 **Rhy. Fig. 2** — **End Rhy. Fig. 2**

mf
P.M. — — — — — — — — — — — — ¬

Gtr. 1: w/ Rhy. Fig. 2
Gtr. 3: w/ Riff A (3 times)

fad - ed, not jad - ed, just a kid with a pad and a pen and a big im - ag - i - na - tion.
hear no cry - in' ass bitch - in' from me, like there seems to be on ev - 'ry - bod - y's C. D. So just

* Gtr. 1: w/ Rhy. Fig. 2 (2 times)

All this I seek, I find. _____ I push the en - ve - lope to the line. _____
sit back and re - lax and let me have your head for a min - ute, I can

Gtr. 4 (dist.) **Riff B** — **End Riff B**

f
Harm. — — — — — — ¬
** w/ delay

* *f* , w/o P.M.

**Set for sixty-fourth note regeneration w/ multiple repeats.

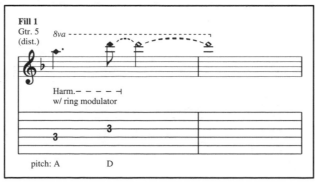

Fill 1
Gtr. 5 (dist.)
8va - - - - - - - - - - - - - - - ¬

Harm. — — — — ¬
w/ ring modulator

pitch: A   D

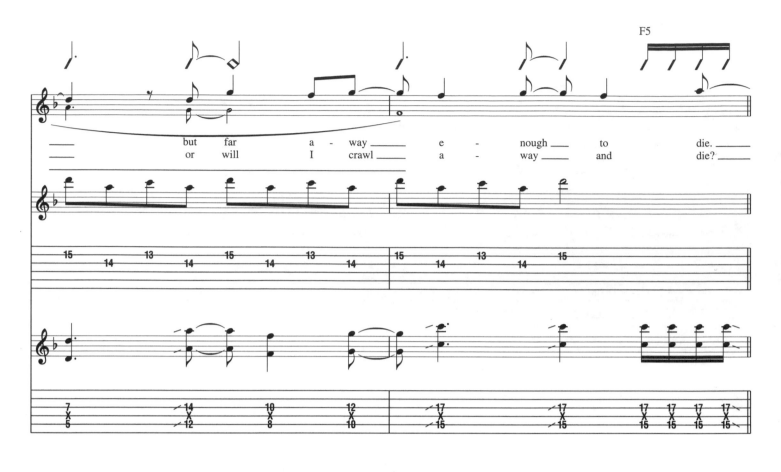

but far   a - way   e -   nough   to   die.
or will   I crawl   a -   way   and   die?

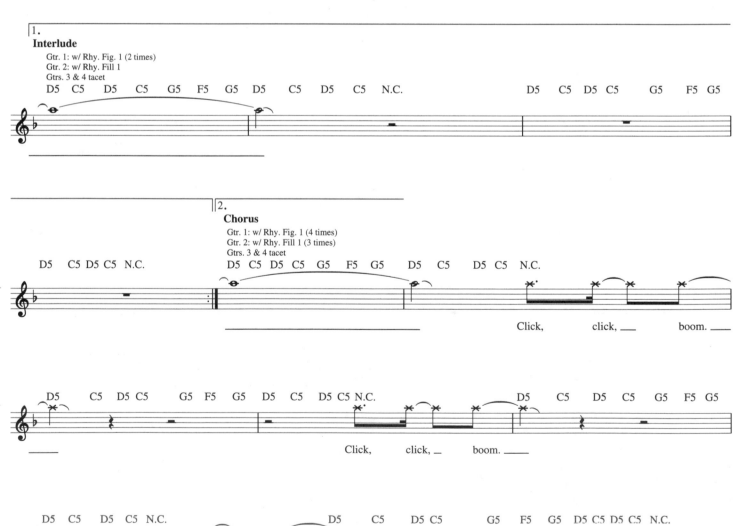

1.
Interlude
Gtr. 1: w/ Rhy. Fig. 1 (2 times)
Gtr. 2: w/ Rhy. Fill 1
Gtrs. 3 & 4 tacet

D5   C5   D5   C5   G5   F5   G5   D5   C5   D5   C5   N.C.   D5   C5   D5   C5   G5   F5   G5

2.
Chorus
Gtr. 1: w/ Rhy. Fig. 1 (4 times)
Gtr. 2: w/ Rhy. Fill 1 (3 times)
Gtrs. 3 & 4 tacet

D5   C5 D5 C5   N.C.   D5   C5 D5   C5   G5   F5   G5   D5   C5   D5 C5   N.C.

Click,   click, ___ boom. ___

D5   C5   D5 C5   G5 F5   G5   D5   C5   D5 C5 N.C.   D5   C5   D5   C5   G5   F5   G5

Click,   click, ___ boom. ___

D5   C5   D5 C5   N.C.   D5   C5   D5 C5   G5   F5   G5   D5 C5 D5 C5 N.C.

Click,   click, ___ boom. ___

Clint Eastwood

Words and Music by 2D, Murdoc Niccals and Teren Delvon Jones

© 2001 GORILLAZ and HAPPY HEMP MUSIC
All Rights for GORILLAZ Assigned to EMI MUSIC PUBLISHING LTD.
All Rights for EMI MUSIC PUBLISHING LTD. in the United States and Canada Controlled and Administered by EMI BLACKWOOD MUSIC INC.
All Rights for HAPPY HEMP MUSIC in the United States and Canada Controlled and
Administered by UNIVERSAL - POLYGRAM INTERNATIONAL PUBLISHING, INC.
All Rights Reserved   International Copyright Secured   Used by Permission

Verse

Gtr. 1: w/ Rhy. Fig. 1 (1 1/2 times)

1. Fi - nal - ly some-one let me out - ta my cage. _ Now, time for me is noth-ing 'cause I'm count-in' no age. _ Now, I

could-n't be there, _ now you should-n't be scared. _ I'm good at re - pairs _ and I'm un - der each snare. _ In - tan -

- gi - ble, bet you did - n't think so, I com-mand you to. Pan - o - ram - ic view, look, I'll make it all man - ag - a - ble.

Pick and choose, sit and lose, all you dif - 'rent crews. Chicks and dudes, who you think is real - ly kick - in' tunes?

Gtr. 1

𝄋 Gtr. 1: w/ Rhy. Fig. 1 (1 1/2 times)

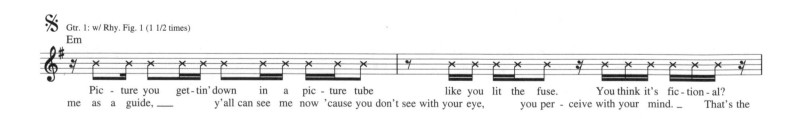

Pic - ture you get-tin' down in a pic - ture tube like you lit the fuse. You think it's fic - tion - al?
me as a guide, ___ y'all can see me now 'cause you don't see with your eye, you per - ceive with your mind. _ That's the

Mys - ti - cal? May - be. Spir - i - tual, hear - a - ble what ap-pears in you's a clear - er view when you're too cra - zy.
in - ner, so I'm a stick a - round with Russ _ and be a men - tor, bust a few rhymes so moth - er fuck - ers re -

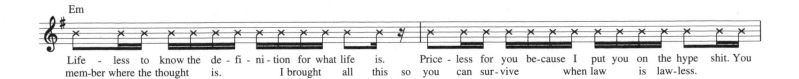

Life - less to know the de - fi - ni - tion for what life is.
mem-ber where the thought is.

Price - less for you be-cause I put you on the hype shit. You
I brought all this so you can sur-vive when law is law-less.

To Coda

N.C.

like it? Gun-smok-in' righ-teous with one to-ken. Psy-chic a-mong those, pos-sess you with one go.
Feel - in's, sen-sa-tions that you thought was dead. No squeal - in', re-mem-ber that it's all in your head.

I ain't

Gtr. 1

Rhy. Fill 1

End Rhy. Fill 1

Chorus

Gtr. 1: w/ Rhy. Fig. 1 (2 times)

Em

hap - py,   I'm feel-ing glad. __ I got sun - shine   in a bag. __ I'm

* Gtr. 2

Riff A

End Riff A

mf

* Melodica arr. for gtr.

Gtr. 2: w/ Riff A (2 times)

F/C

use - less,   but not for long. __ The fu - ture   is com - in' on. __ I ain't

Em

hap - py,   I'm feel-ing glad. __ I got sun - shine   in a bag. __ I'm

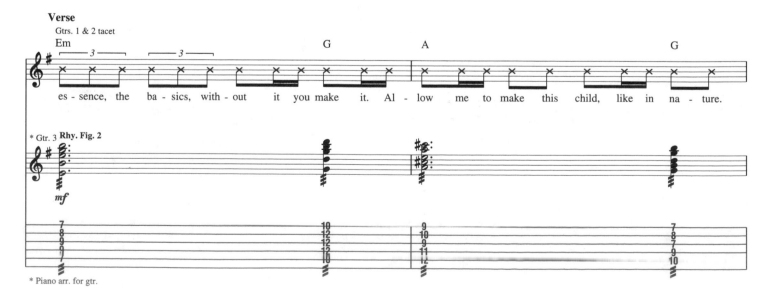

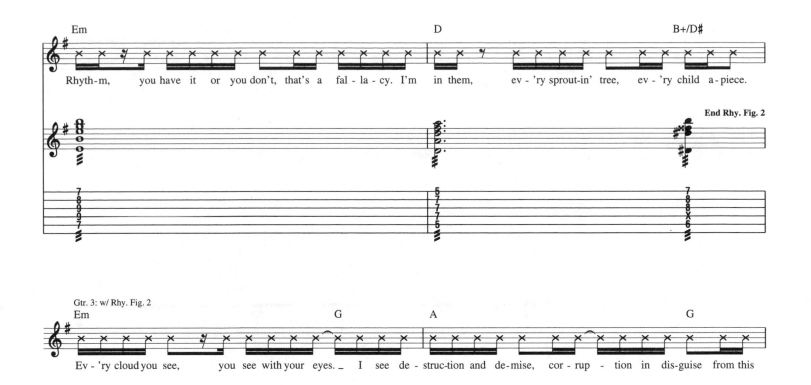

Rhyth-m, you have it or you don't, that's a fal-la-cy. I'm in them, ev-'ry sprout-in' tree, ev-'ry child a-piece.

End Rhy. Fig. 2

Gtr. 3: w/ Rhy. Fig. 2

Ev-'ry cloud you see, you see with your eyes. _ I see de-struc-tion and de-mise, cor-rup-tion in dis-guise from this

D.S. al Coda

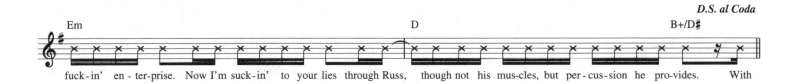

fuck-in' en-ter-prise. Now I'm suck-in' to your lies through Russ, though not his mus-cles, but per-cus-sion he pro-vides. With

⊕ **Coda**

Chorus

Gtr. 1: w/ Rhy. Fig. 1 (2 1/2 times)

hap-py, I'm feel-ing glad. _ I got sun-shine in a bag. _ I'm

use-less, but not for long. _ The fu-ture is com-in' on. _ I ain't

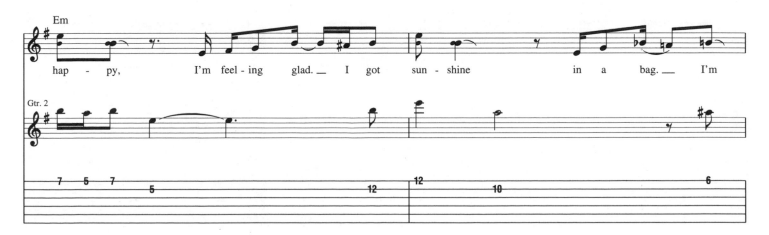

hap-py, I'm feel-ing glad. _ I got sun-shine in a bag. _ I'm

Outro Melodica Solo

* Set delay for dotted eighth-note regeneration w/ multiple repeats.

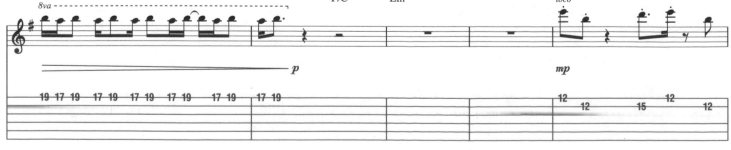

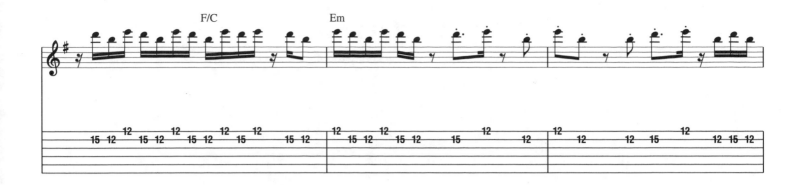

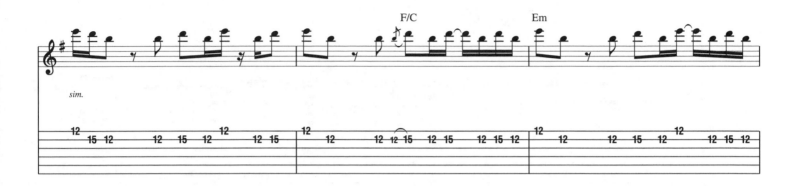

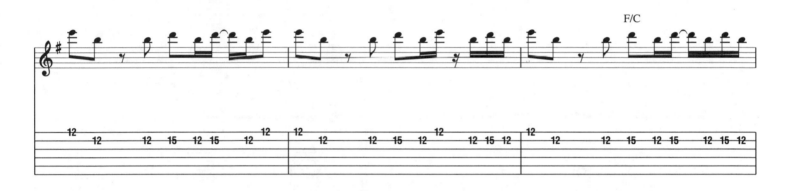

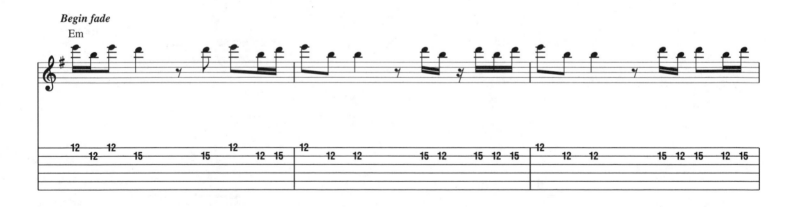

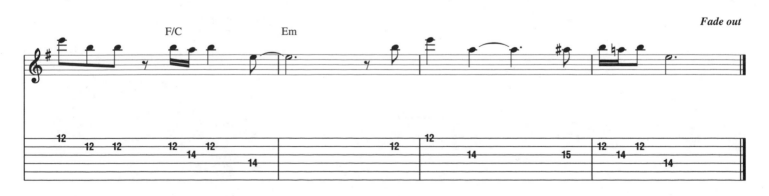

Dig In

Words and Music by Lenny Kravitz

Copyright © 2001 Miss Bessie Music (ASCAP)
International Copyright Secured   All Rights Reserved

Pre-Chorus

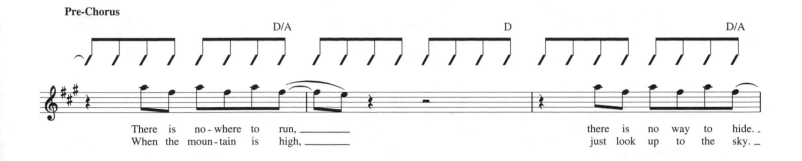

There is no-where to run, _____ there is no way to hide. _
When the moun-tain is high, _____ just look up to the sky. _

_____ Don't let it beat you, say "nice to meet you" and fight. _
_____ Ask God to teach you, then per - se - vere with a smile. _

% **Chorus**
1st & 3rd times, Gtr. 1: w/ Rhy. Fig. 1 (1 3/4 times)
2nd time, Gtr. 1: w/ Rhy. Fig. 1 (4 times)

Yeah, yeah, yeah! Once you dig in, _____

you'll find you're com - ing out the oth - er side. And once you dig in, ___

To Coda ⊕
Gtr. 1: w/ Rhy. Fill 1

___ you'll find you'll have _____ your - self a good time.

_____ your - self a good time. Once you dig in, _____ you'll find you're com -

CHARLES CITY PUBLIC LIBRARY
106 Milwaukee Mall
Charles City, IA 50616-2281

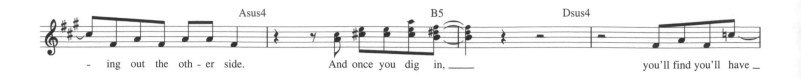

-ing out the oth-er side.   And once you dig in, ____   you'll find you'll have ___

Guitar Solo

Gtr. 1: w/ Rhy. Fig. 1 (2 times)

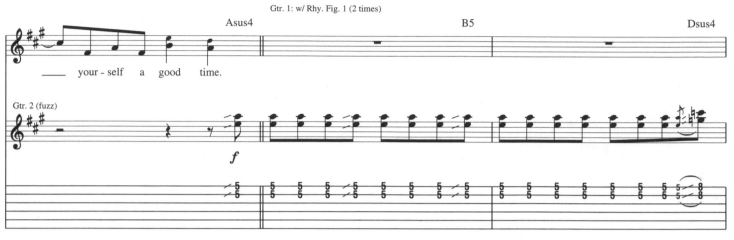

____ your-self   a   good   time.

Gtr. 2 (fuzz)

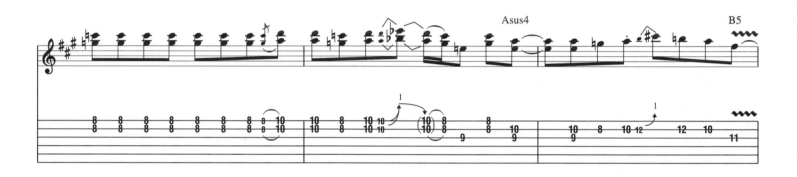

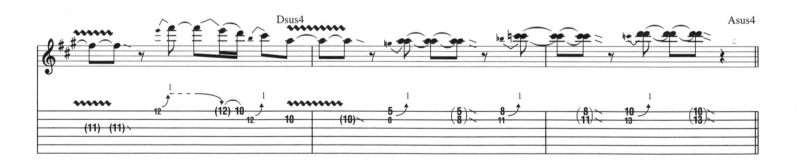

Chorus

Gtr. 2 tacet   Gtr. 1 tacet

Once you dig in, ____   you'll find you're com - ing out the oth-er side.

36

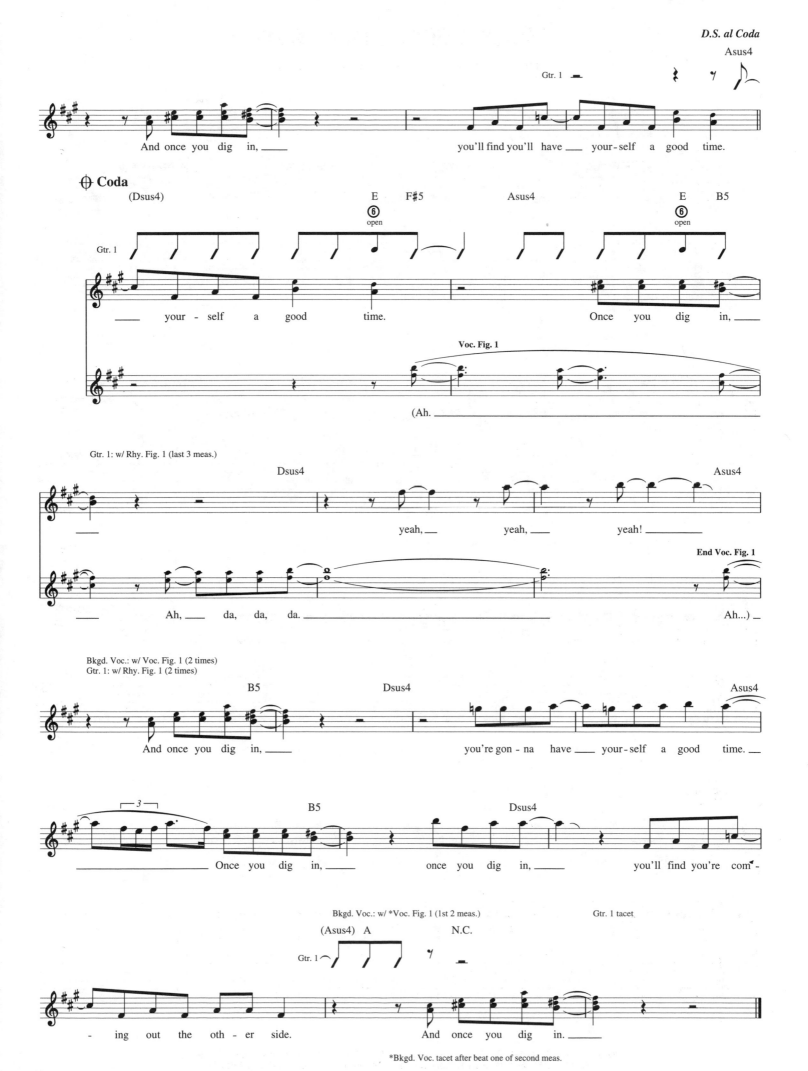

Gets Me Through

Words and Music by Ozzy Osbourne and Tim Palmer

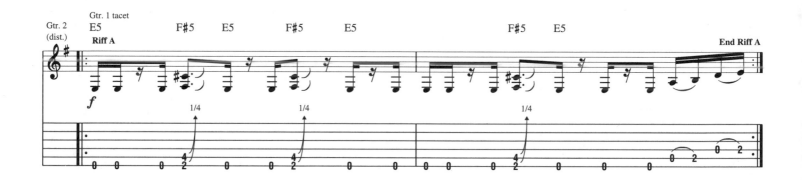

© 2001 EMI VIRGIN MUSIC INC., MONOWISE LTD., PARKERSONGS MUSIC and TP SONGS
All Rights for MONOWISE LTD. Controlled and Administered by EMI VIRGIN MUSIC INC.
All Rights Reserved   International Copyright Secured   Used by Permission

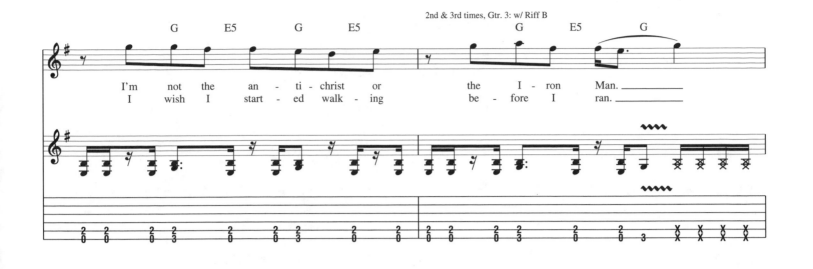

I'm not the an - ti - christ or the I - ron Man. _____
I wish I start - ed walk - ing be - fore I ran. _____

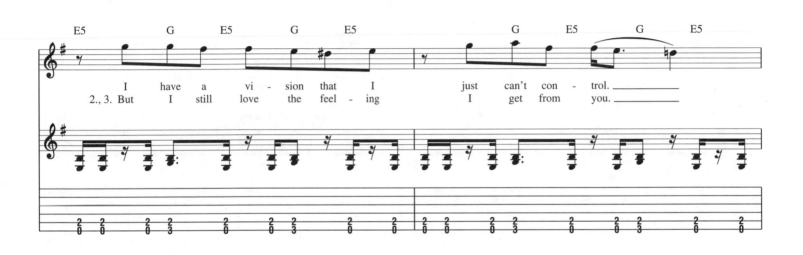

I have a vi - sion that I just can't con - trol. _____
2., 3. But I still love the feel - ing I get from you. _____

To Coda ⊕

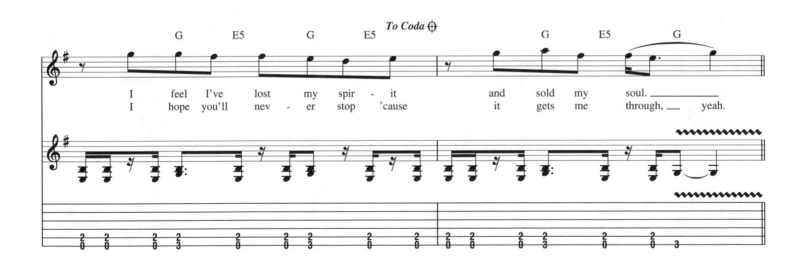

I feel I've lost my spir - it and sold my soul. _____
I hope you'll nev - er stop 'cause it gets me through, ___ yeah.

Riff B
Gtr. 3 (slight dist.)

mf
let ring throughout
w/ panning effect

39

Interlude

Gtr. 2: w/ Riff A (2 times)

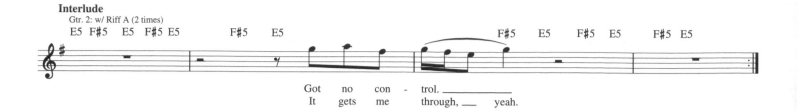

Got no con - trol. ___
It gets me through, ___ yeah.

Bridge

The feel-ings that ___ I ___ hide ___ be - hind. ___ Some-times re - al - i - ty's ___ un - kind. ___

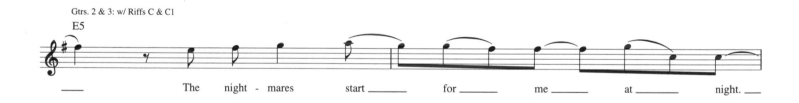

Gtrs. 2 & 3: w/ Riffs C & C1

___ The night - mares start _____ for _____ me _____ at _____ night. ___

Gtrs. 2 & 3: w/ Fill 1 & Rhy. Fill 1

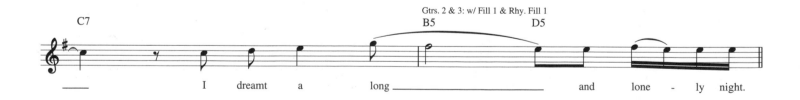

___ I dreamt a long _____ and lone - ly night.

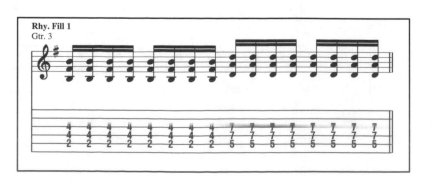

Guitar Solo

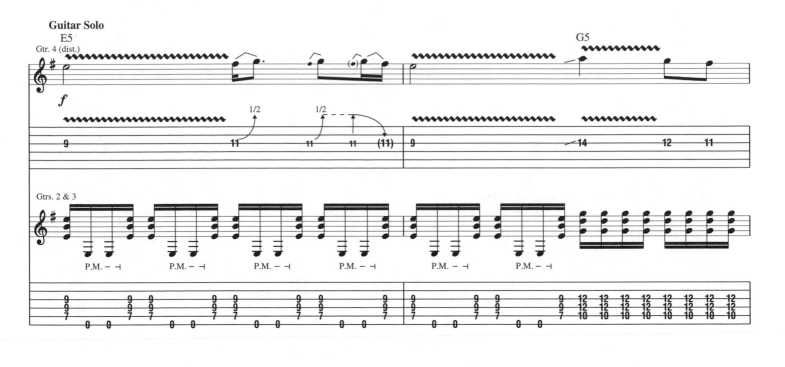

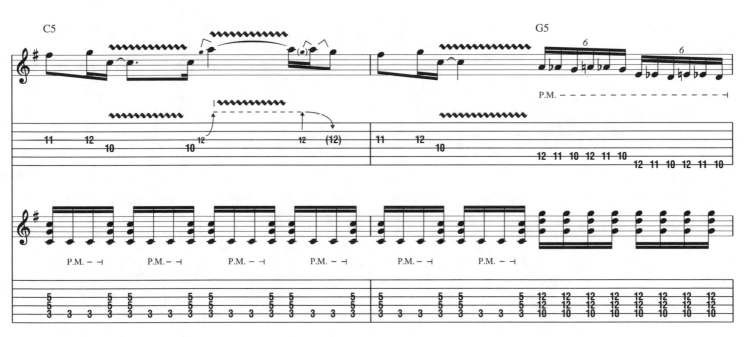

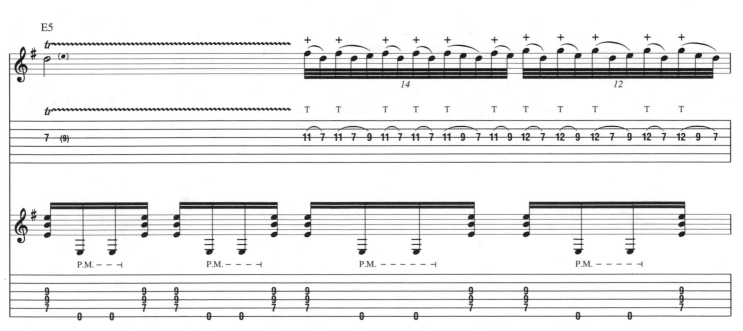

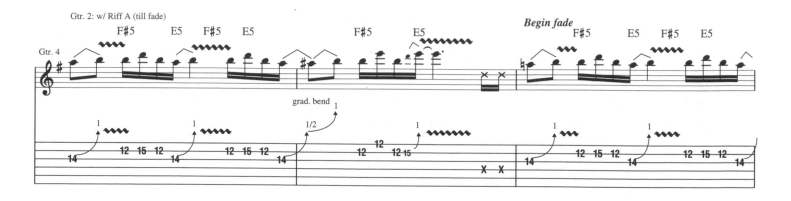

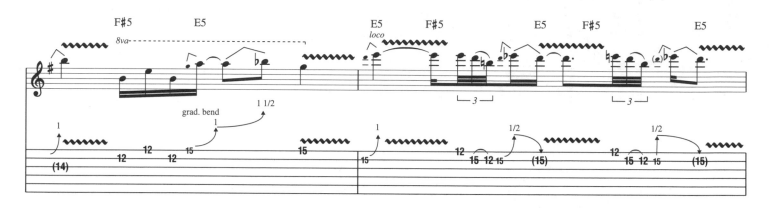

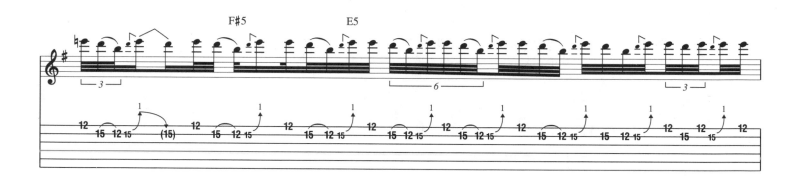

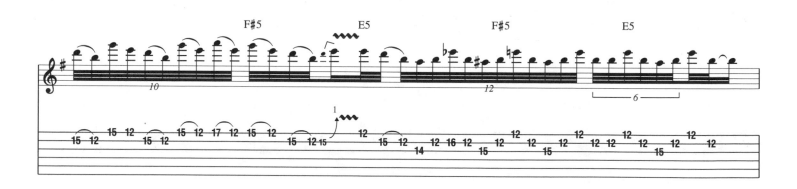

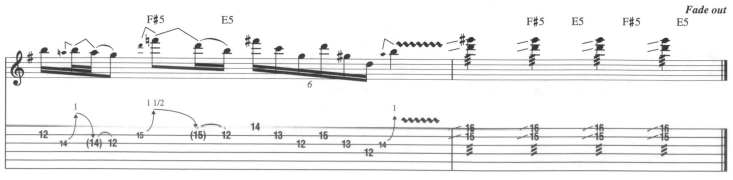

In Too Deep

Words and Music by Sum 41

*Chord symbols reflect implied harmony.

© 2001 EMI APRIL MUSIC (CANADA) LTD., RECTUM RENOVATOR MUSIC and BUNK ROCK MUSIC, INC.
All Rights for RECTUM RENOVATOR MUSIC in the U.S. Controlled and Administered by EMI APRIL MUSIC INC.
All Rights for BUNK ROCK MUSIC, INC. Administered by CHRYSALIS MUSIC
All Rights Reserved   International Copyright Secured   Used by Permission

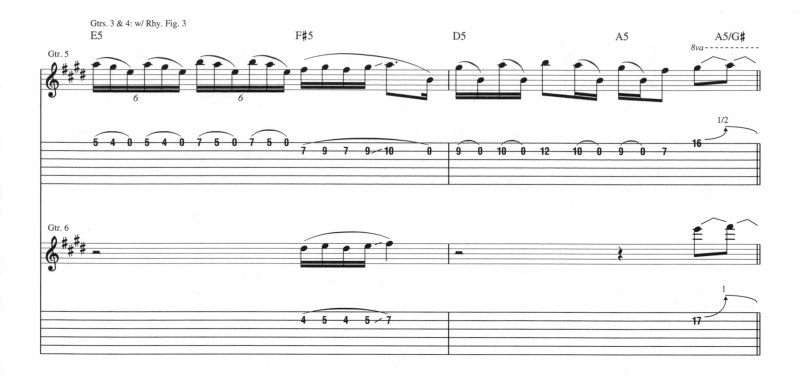

Bridge

I can't sit back and __ won - der why. __ It took so long for __ this to die. __

And I hate it when you fake it. You can't hide it, you might as well em-brace it.

So be-lieve me, it's not eas-y. It seems that some-thin's tell-in' me I'm

Chorus

in too deep and I'm try'n' to keep up a-bove in my head in-stead

Lateralus

**Words and Music by Maynard James Keenan, Adam Jones,
Daniel Carey and Justin Chancellor**

G5

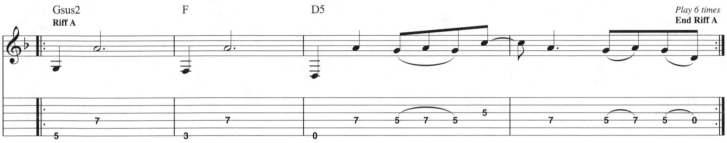

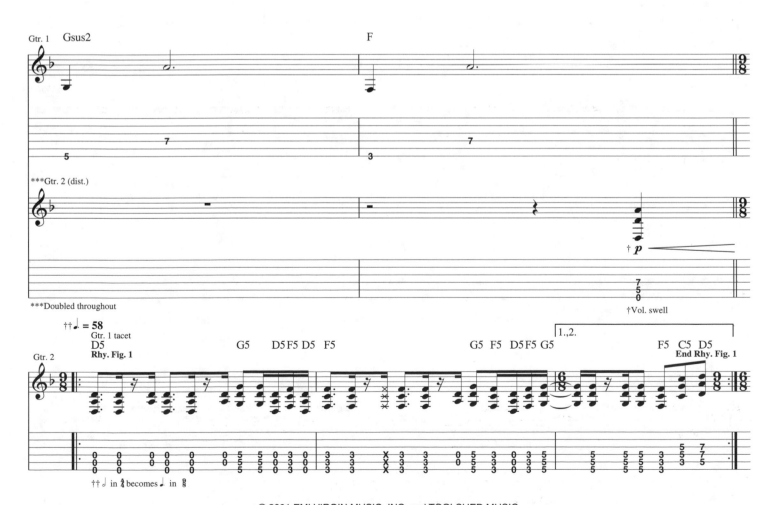

© 2001 EMI VIRGIN MUSIC, INC. and TOOLSHED MUSIC
All Rights Controlled and Administered by EMI VIRGIN MUSIC, INC.
All Rights Reserved   International Copyright Secured   Used by Permission

Verse

1. Black then white are all I see in my in-fan-cy. Red and yel-low then came to be, reach-in' out to me, lets me see.

As be-low, so a-bove and be-yond I im-ag-ine. Drawn be-yond the lines of rea-son, push the en-ve-lope, watch it bend.

Interlude

Chorus
Gtr. 2: w/ Rhy. Fig. 1 (2 times)
Gtr. 4 tacet

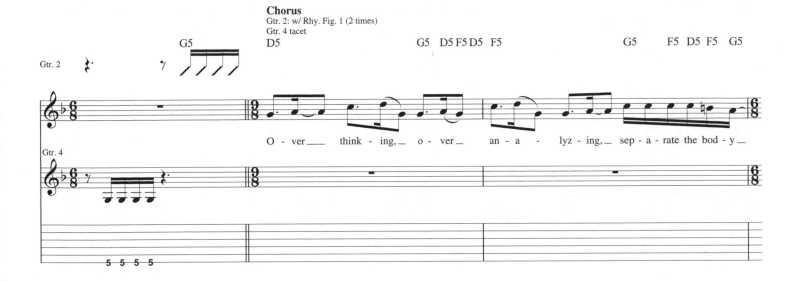

O-ver___ think-ing,___ o-ver___ an-a-lyz-ing,___ sep-a-rate the bod-y___

___ from the mind.___ With-er-ing my___ in-tu-i-tion, miss-ing___ op-por-tu-ni-

-ties and I___must feed my___ will___ to___ feel___ my mo-ment.___ Draw-ing___ way out-side

Gtr. 2 **Rhy. Fig. 2**

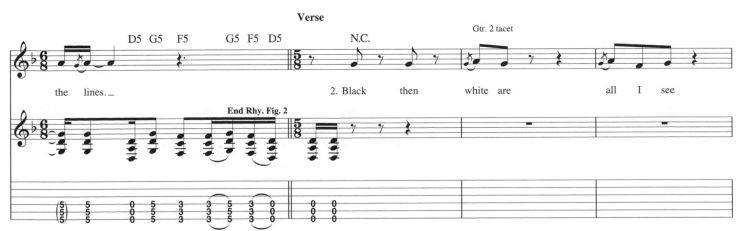

Verse

the lines.___

2. Black then white are all I see

Gtr. 2 tacet

End Rhy. Fig. 2

in my in-fan-cy. Red and yel-low then came to be, reach-in' out to me, lets me see

there is so much more and beck-ons me

to look through to these in-fi-nite pos-si-bil-i-ties. ___

Gtr. 4: w/ Riff C (2 times)

As be-low, so a-bove and be-yond I im-ag-ine. Drawn out-side the lines

of rea-son, push the en-ve-lope, watch it bend.

Interlude
Gtr. 4: w/ Riff D (2 times)

Chorus
Gtr. 2: w/ Rhy. Fig. 1

O-ver___ think-ing,___ o-ver___ an-a-lyz-ing,___ sep-a-rate the bod-y ___

Gtr. 2

Gtr. 2: w/ Rhy. Fig. 2

___ from the mind. ___ With-er-ing my in-tu-i-tion, ___ leav-ing___ op-por-tu-ni-

Guitar Solo

- ties be-hind. ___

Gtr. 5 (dist.)

f

w/ wah-wah as filter

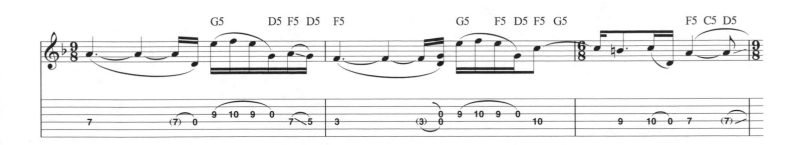

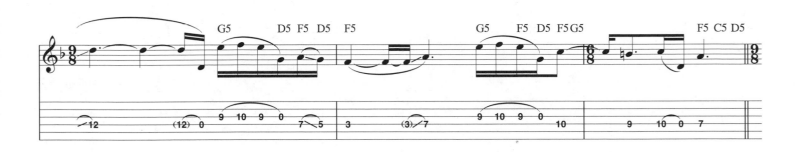

Bridge

Feed_ my_ will to_ feel_ this_ mo - ment,_ urg - ing_ me to_____ cross the line._

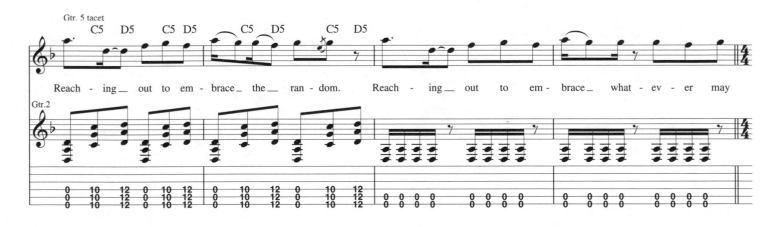

Reach - ing_ out to em - brace_ the_ ran - dom. Reach - ing_ out to em - brace_ what - ev - er may

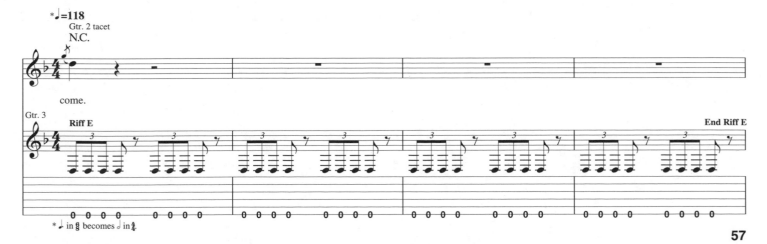

come.

57

swing on the spi - ral, _____ to   swing_ on the spi - ral, _____ to... _____

Gtr. 1

Swing   on   the   spi - ral _ of _   our _____ di - vin - i - ty _ and _

still   be   a   hu - man. _____

With my_ feet_ up-on the_ ground, I_ lose my-self_ be-tween the_ sounds_ and

o-pen_ wide_ to suck it_ in._ I feel it_ move a-cross my_ skin._ I'm

reach-in'_ up_ and reach-in' out. I'm reach-in'_ for_ the_ ran-dom_ or_ what-

ev - er_ will_ be - wil - der_ me, what - ev - er_ will_ be - wil - der_ me._ And

fol - low - ing__ our_ will and_ wind,_ we may just_ go__ where no_ one's_ been._ We'll

ride the_ spi - ral to the_ end__ and may just_ go__ where no_ one's_ been._

Spi - ral_ out, keep go - ing._ Spi - ral_ out, keep go - ing._

Spi - ral__ out, keep go - ing._ Spi - ral_ out, keep go - ing._

Left Behind

Words and Music by M. Shawn Crahan, Paul Gray, Nathan Jordison, Corey Taylor, Chris Fehn, Nick Thompson, Sid Wilson and James Root

Drop D tuning, down 1 1/2 steps:
(low to high) B–F#–B–E–G#–C#

Intro

Moderately fast ♩ = 150

© 2001 EMI APRIL MUSIC INC. and MUSIC THAT MUSIC
All Rights Controlled and Administered by EMI APRIL MUSIC INC.
All Rights Reserved   International Copyright Secured   Used by Permission

Bridge

We let it all slip a - way!

We let it all slip a - way!

Photograph

Words and Music by Rivers Cuomo

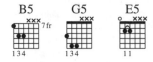

* Chord symbols reflect basic harmony.

** Doubled by Gtr. 2 on repeat.

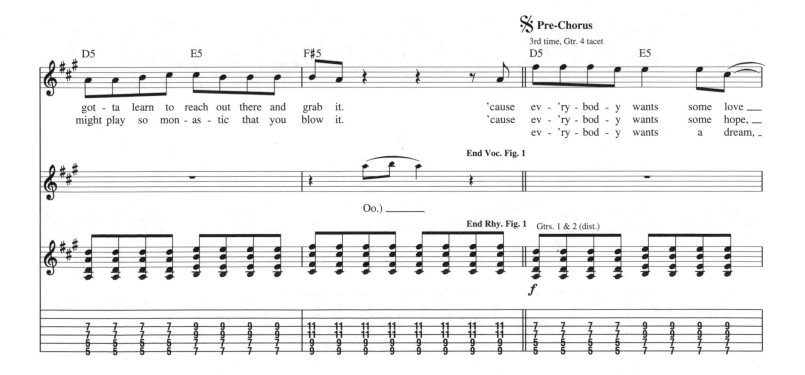

Copyright © 2001 E.O. Smith Music
International Copyright Secured   All Rights Reserved

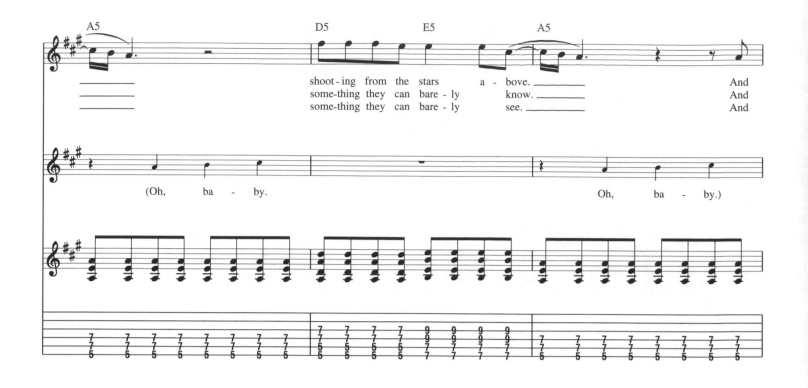

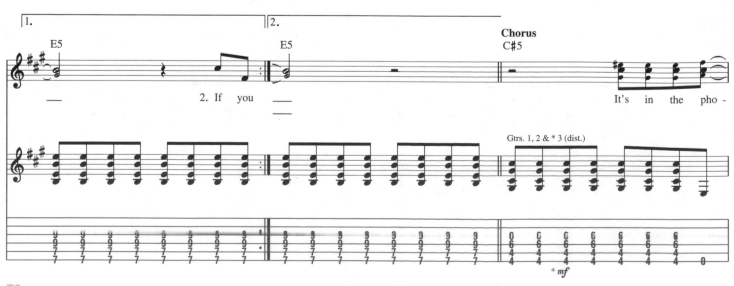

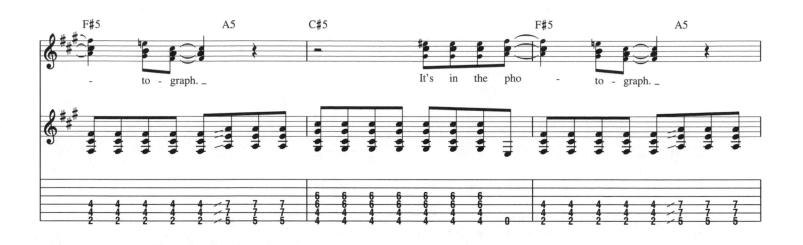

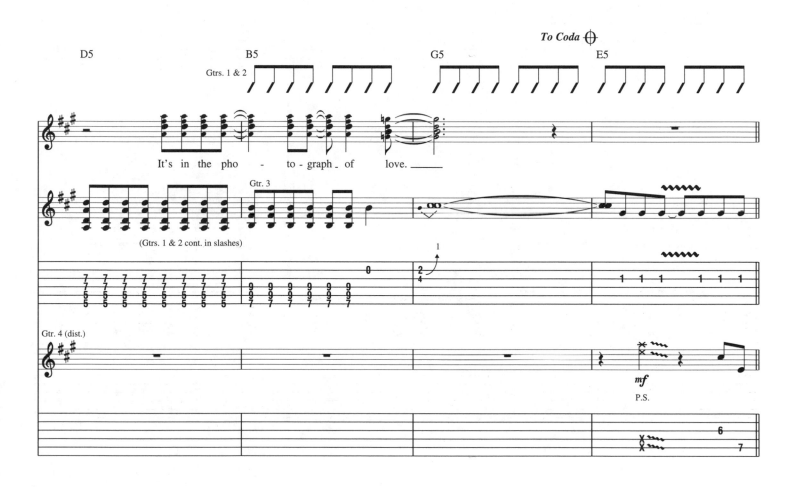

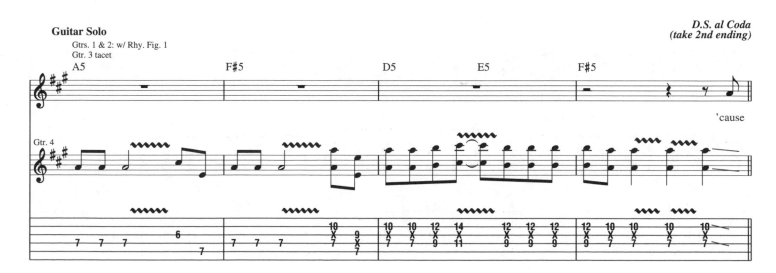

Coda

Outro-Verse

Bkgd. Voc.: w/ Voc. Fig. 1
Gtr. 3 tacet

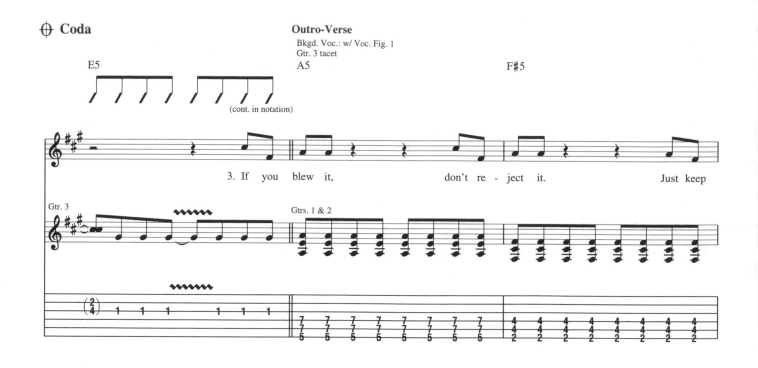

3. If you blew it, don't re - ject it. Just keep

Bkgd. Voc.: w/ Voc. Fig. 1 (last 2 meas.) (3 times)

draw - ing up the plans and re - e - rect it. Just keep draw - ing up the plans and re - e -

w/ sound effects
& Voc. ad lib.

rect it. Just keep draw - ing up the plans and re - e - rect it.

Superman (It's Not Easy)

Words and Music by John Ondrasik

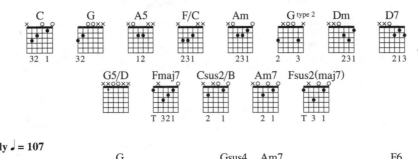

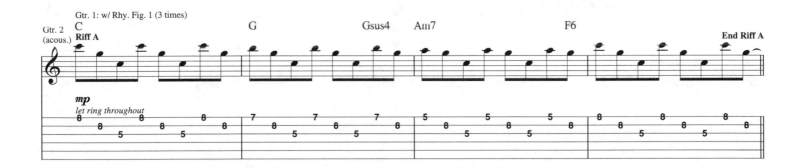

*Piano arr. for gtr.

**Chord symbols reflect implied harmony.

1. I can't stand___ to fly,_____ I'm not that___ na - ive.

I'm just out___ to find____ the bet - ter part of ___ me. I'm more than a bird.___

© 2000 EMI BLACKWOOD MUSIC INC. and FIVE FOR FIGHTING MUSIC
All Rights Controlled and Administered by EMI BLACKWOOD MUSIC INC.
All Rights Reserved   International Copyright Secured   Used by Permission

Chorus

I'm more than a plane,__ I'm more than some pret-ty face__ be-side a train. And it's not__ ea-

Gtr. 2

Gtr. 3
(acous.)

mp
let ring throughout

-sy to ___ be ___ me. ___

2. I

(cont. in slashes)

*T = Thumb on 6th string.

Verse

Rhy. Fig. 2

Gtr. 2

wish that __ I __ could __ cry, __ fall __ up - on my __ knees.

Gtr. 3

76

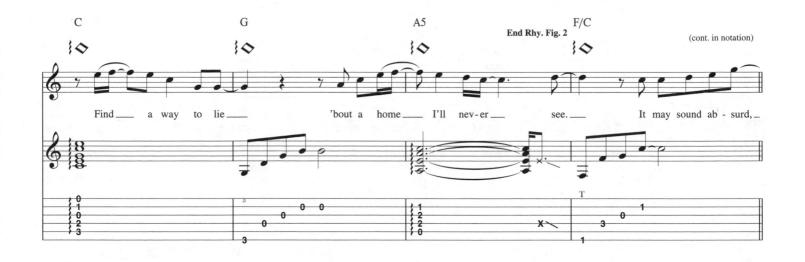

Find__ a way to lie__ 'bout a home__ I'll nev-er__ see.__ It may sound ab - surd,

Chorus

__ but don't be na - ive,__ e - ven he - roes have__ the right to bleed. I may be dis - turbed,__

__ but won't you con - cede,__ e - ven he - roes have__ the right to dream. And it's not__ ea -

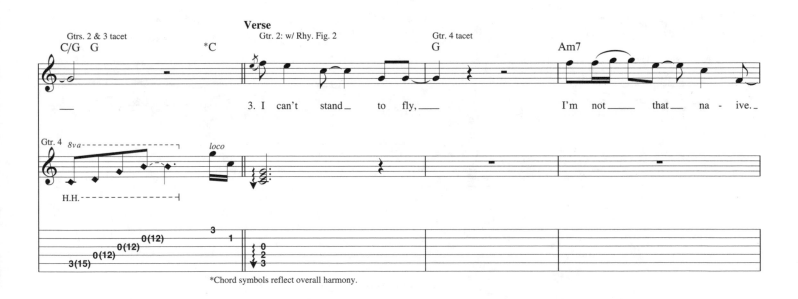

*Chord symbols reflect overall harmony.

Chorus

I'm on-ly a man in a sil-ly red sheet, dig-ging for kryp-ton-ite on this one

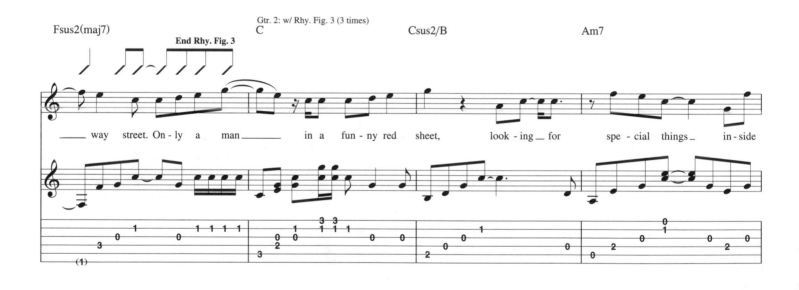

way street. On-ly a man in a fun-ny red sheet, look-ing for spe-cial things in-side

of me, in-side of me, in-side of me.

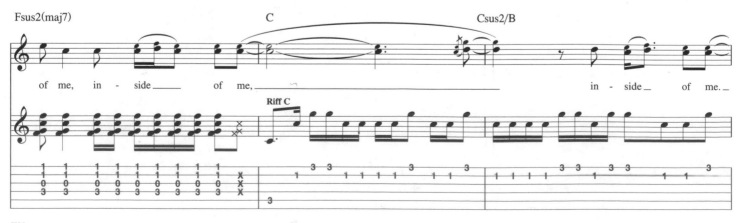

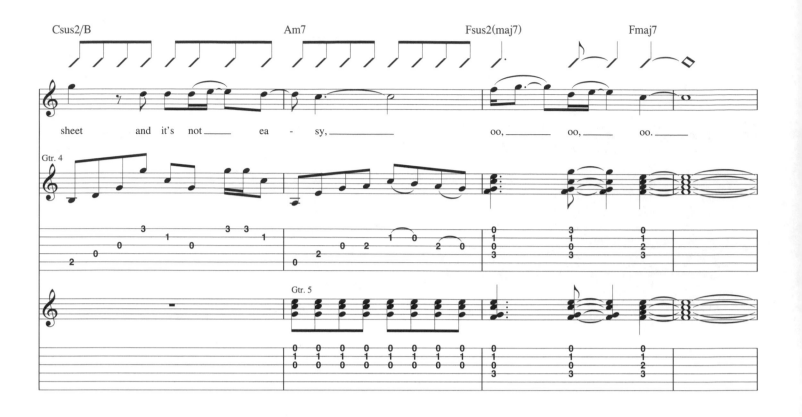

sheet   and   it's   not____   ea - sy,_____   oo,_____   oo,_____   oo.____

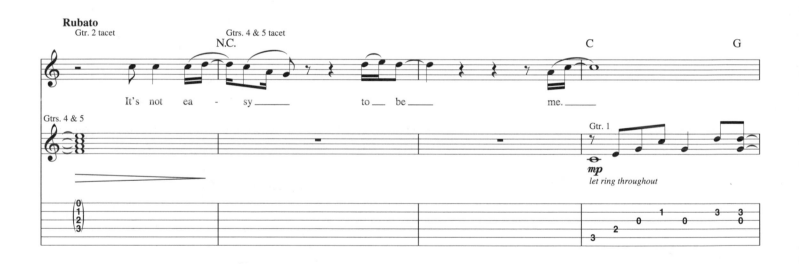

It's   not   ea - sy_____   to __ be___   me.____

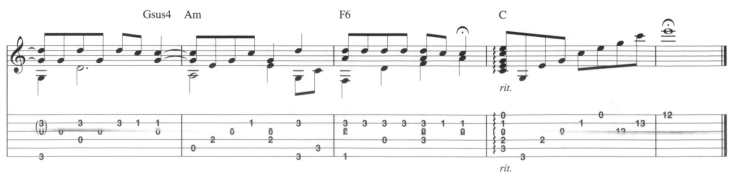

Wherever You Will Go

Words and Music by Alex Band and Aaron Kamin

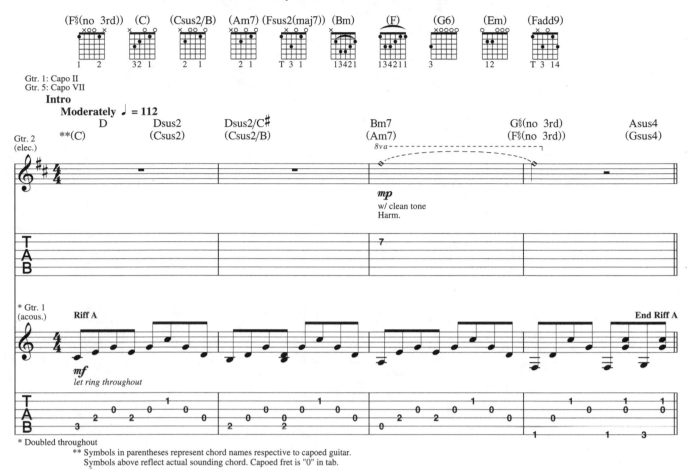

Gtr. 1: Capo II
Gtr. 5: Capo VII

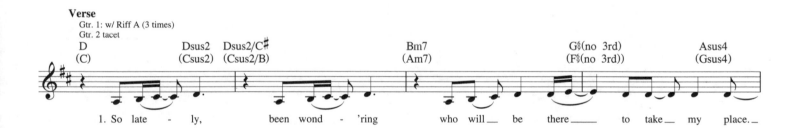

* Doubled throughout

** Symbols in parentheses represent chord names respective to capoed guitar.
Symbols above reflect actual sounding chord. Capoed fret is "0" in tab.

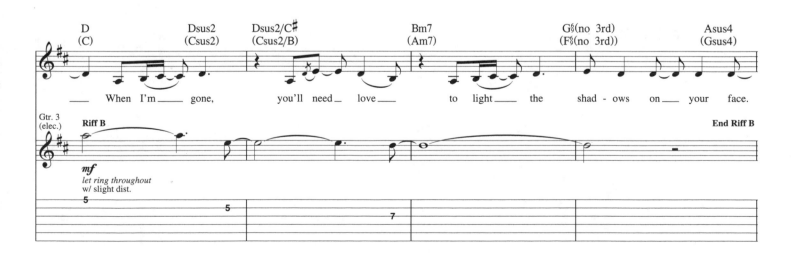

Copyright © 2001 by Careers-BMG Music Publishing, Inc., Alex Band Music and Amedeo Music
All Rights Administered by Careers-BMG Music Publishing, Inc.
International Copyright Secured All Rights Reserved

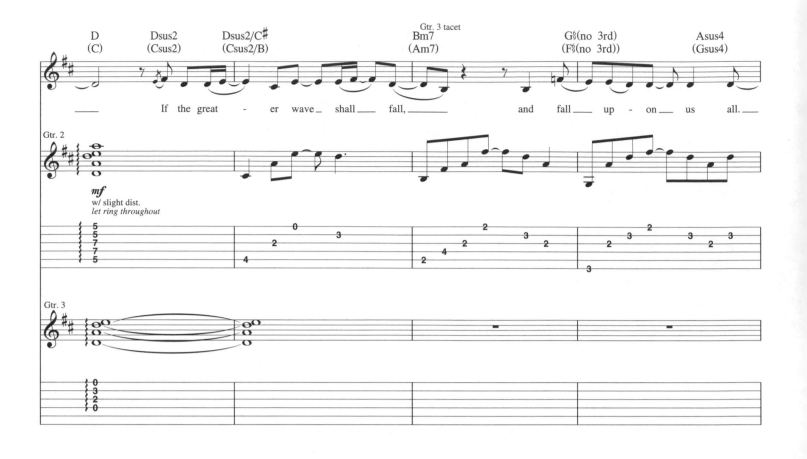

If the great - er wave_ shall_ fall,_____ and fall_ up - on us all.___

Then be - tween___ the sand_ and stone___ could you make_ it on_ your own?_

Chorus

If I _____ could, then I _____ would, I'll go wher - ev - er ___ you ___ will go. ___

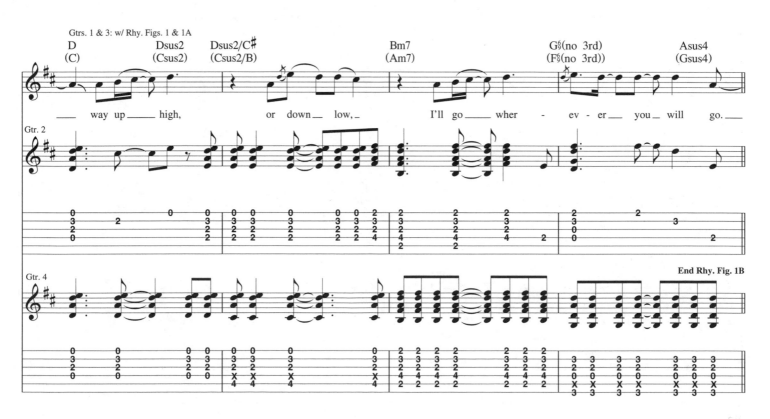

___ way up ___ high, or down ___ low, ___ I'll go ___ wher - ev - er ___ you ___ will go. ___

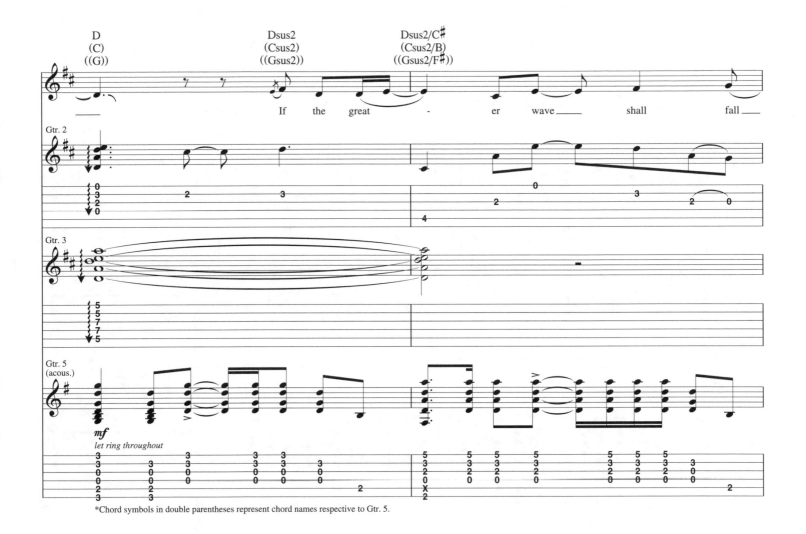

*Chord symbols in double parentheses represent chord names respective to Gtr. 5.

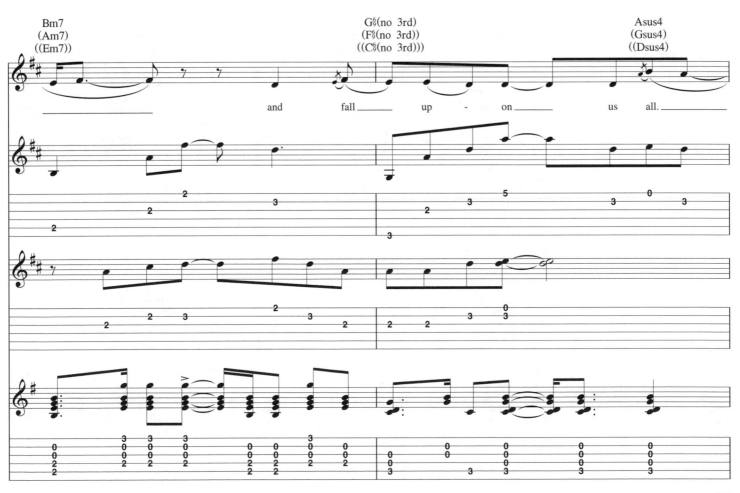

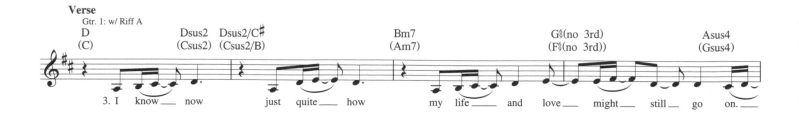

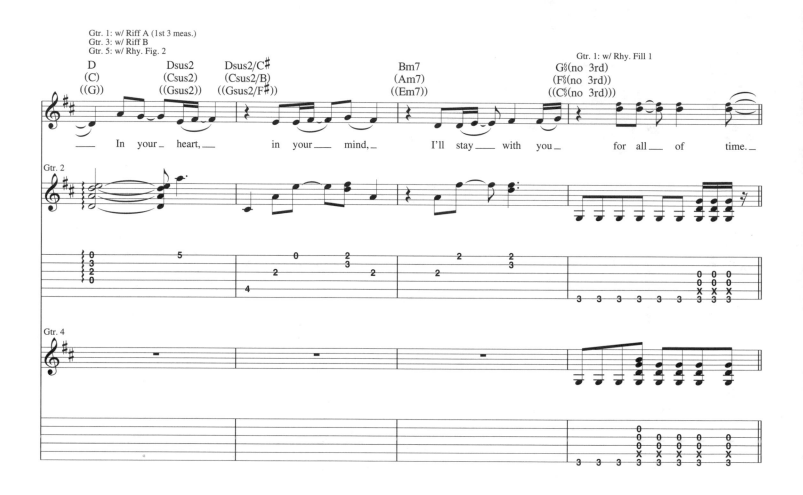

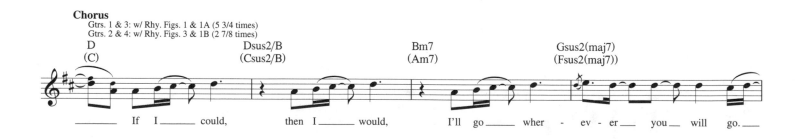

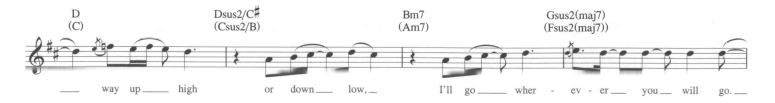

Wish You Were Here

Words and Music by Brandon Boyd, Michael Einziger, Alex Katunich, Jose Pasillas II and Chris Kilmore

© 2001 EMI APRIL MUSIC INC. and HUNGLIKEYORA MUSIC
All Rights Controlled and Administered by EMI APRIL MUSIC INC.
All Rights Reserved   International Copyright Secured   Used by Permission

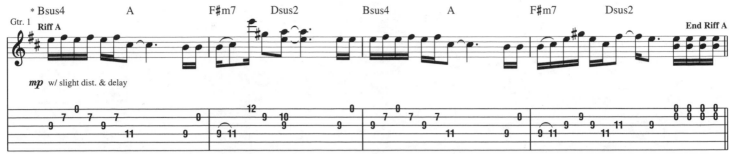

Gtr. 1 · Riff A · End Riff A

mp w/ slight dist. & delay

*Chord symbols reflect overall harmony.

Verse

Gtr. 1: w/ Riff A (1 1/2 times)

Bsus4 · A · F#m7 · Dsus2

1. I dig ____ my toes ____ in - to ____ the sand. ____
2. I lay ____ my head ____ on - to ____ the sand. ____

Bsus4 · A · F#m7 · Dsus2

The o - cean looks __ like a thou - sand dia - monds __ strewn a - cross __ a blue plane.
The sky __ re - sem - bles a back - lit can - o - py _____ with holes __ punched in it.

Bsus4 · A · F#m7 · Dsus2

I lean ____ a - gainst ____ the wind, __ pre - tend - in' I ____ am weight - less.
I'm count - ing U. __ F. O.'s. __ I sig - nal them with, __ through my lad - der,

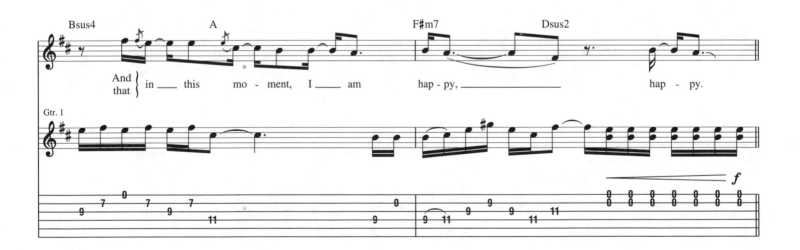

Bsus4 · A · F#m7 · Dsus2

And that { in ____ this mo - ment, I ____ am hap - py, _____ hap - py.

Gtr. 1

f

Chorus

Gtrs. 1 & 2: w/ Rhy. Fig. 2 (2 times) · Gtr. 3: w/ Rhy. Fig. 3

Asus2 · E5 · B5/F# · D5/A · E5 · Asus2 · E5

I ____ wish you were here. ____ I ____

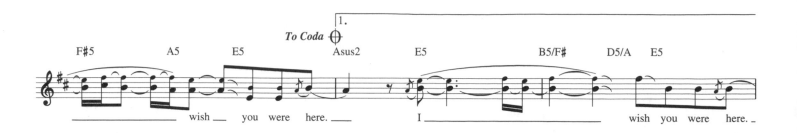

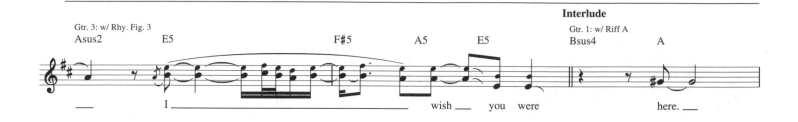

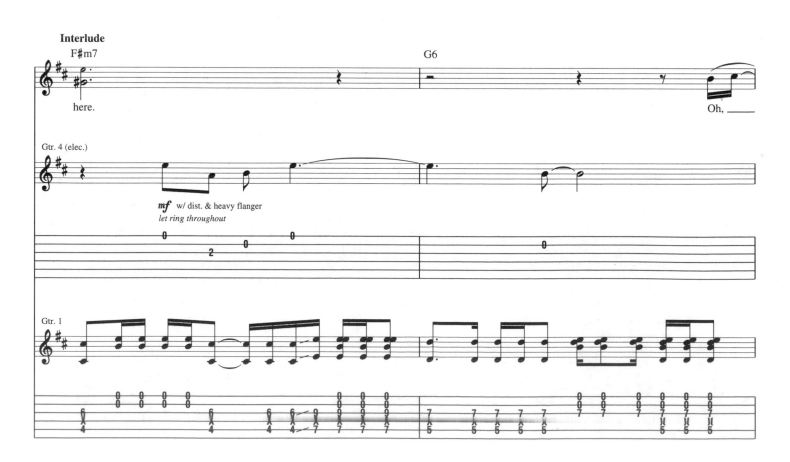

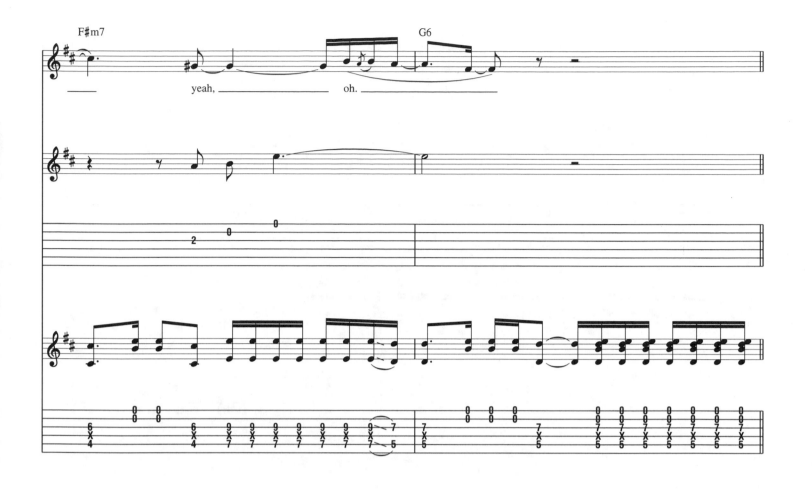

yeah, _____ oh. _____

Bridge

The world's _ a rol - ler coast - er,   and I ____ am not _ strapped in. ___

Oo, may-be I should hold _ with care, _ but my hand's _ are in _ the, in _ the air _ say-

Gtr. 1: w/ Rhy. Fig. 1
Gtr. 4 tacet

D.S. al Coda

ing,   "I _____   wish you were here. _____ I _____   wish _ you were..."

⊕ Coda

Gtrs. 1 & 2: w/ Rhy. Fig. 2

_____ I _____   wish   you   were

Gtr. 3: w/ Rhy. Fig. 3

here, _____   wish _   you   were   here.

Gtrs. 1 & 2

U0897396

To the Student

We have provided you with this *Speech Preparation Workbook* to use in your public speaking course. In this workbook you will find a variety of forms to help with preparing your self-introductory speech, analyzing your audience, selecting your topics, conducting your research, organizing supporting materials, and outlining your speeches. We have included one copy of each of the outline worksheets and other materials you may need in the course. Because you may decide to use the same design for more than one assignment, make an extra copy of the blank worksheet so that you will have a backup. Make copies of other materials and forms in this workbook so that you will have enough for all of your assignments. Use these workbook materials to make your journey through the realm of public speaking a little easier to navigate.

Checklist for Speech Preparation

Phase I

_____ Select your topic: Focus on something that can be handled within the time constraints of your assignment and the time needed for preparation.

_____ Determine your purpose for speaking. Think clearly about what you want to accomplish with your presentation.

_____ Analyze your audience and speaking situation.

_____ Review your purpose in terms of how it fits with your specific audience and speaking situation.

_____ Reconsider your topic in light of audience and situational factors and your purpose for speaking.

_____ Begin researching your topic. If necessary, refocus your topic and adjust your purpose in light of your research.

Phase II

_____ Develop a preparation outline of the body of your speech.

_____ Check the adequacy of your research in terms of responsible knowledge and sufficient supporting material. Do additional research if it is needed.

_____ Check the organization of your main ideas. Do they flow smoothly? Is the speech easy to follow?

_____ Write an introduction for your speech.

_____ Develop a conclusion for your speech.

_____ Prepare a formal outline which includes transitions and works consulted.

_____ Prepare a key-word outline.

_____ Practice your presentation.

Copyright © Houghton Mifflin Company. All rights reserved.

Learning by Objectives Worksheet

Name: _____

Major: _____

Career aspirations: _____

Person interviewed: _____

1. Objective: _____

   How to reach it: _____

2. Objective: _____

   How to reach it: _____

3. Objective: _____

   How to reach it: _____

4. Objective: _____

   How to reach it: _____

Copyright © Houghton Mifflin Company. All rights reserved.

"How Free Is Too Free?"

Please respond using the following code:

7 = strongly agree
6 = agree
5 = agree somewhat
4 = neutral or not sure
3 = disagree somewhat
2 = disagree
1 = strongly disagree

1 2 3 4 5 6 7   There is too much violence on TV.

1 2 3 4 5 6 7   There is too much sexually explicit content on TV.

1 2 3 4 5 6 7   There is too much intolerance (e.g., racism, sexism, homophobia, or anti-Semitism) on TV.

1 2 3 4 5 6 7   Viewing violent movies causes people to be violent.

1 2 3 4 5 6 7   Sexually explicit materials provide an outlet for bottled-up impulses.

1 2 3 4 5 6 7   Sexually explicit materials lead to rape.

1 2 3 4 5 6 7   Sexually explicit materials lead to the breakdown of morals.

1 2 3 4 5 6 7   The government should restrict blatantly violent, sexually explicit, or intolerant expression on television.

1 2 3 4 5 6 7   The media should restrict unusually violent, sexually explicit, or intolerant expression on television.

1 2 3 4 5 6 7   Unusually violent, sexually explicit, or intolerant expression should not be restricted.

1 2 3 4 5 6 7   Individuals should be free to voice their disapproval of unusually violent, sexually explicit, or intolerant material.

1 2 3 4 5 6 7   One problem with laws against offensive speech is that once certain messages are banned, any material could be banned.

1 2 3 4 5 6 7   Not censoring offensive messages puts many of our cherished values at risk.

1 2 3 4 5 6 7   Campus speech codes will not combat the problems of prejudice and insensitivity to others' beliefs.

1 2 3 4 5 6 7   Leaving censorship up to the media will guarantee that more offensive messages will be permitted.

1 2 3 4 5 6 7   Restrictions on free speech, whether by government or media, threaten our obligation as a democratic society to protect minority views.

1 2 3 4 5 6 7   One good way to deal with racist attitudes on campuses is to encourage open discussions about racial differences.

1 2 3 4 5 6 7   Unlimited free speech carries individual rights to such an extreme that responsibilities to the community are neglected.

Copyright © Houghton Mifflin Company. All rights reserved.

Reading Log

Name: _____   Date: _____

Title (or text chapter): _____

Author (if not from text): _____

Source (if not from text): _____

Applicability to current assignment: _____

_____

_____

_____

_____

_____

Applicability outside of class: _____

_____

_____

_____

_____

Copyright © Houghton Mifflin Company. All rights reserved.

Guidelines for Preparing a Speech of Self-introduction

The speech of self-introduction provides you with an opportunity to develop credibility before your audience. It is a chance for you to be seen as competent, trustworthy, likable, and forceful. Since no one can relate his or her life story in a single speech, you should choose a topic that best defines you (or the person whom you are introducing). Use the Self-awareness Inventory on pp. 6–7 to help you come up with a specific topic for your presentation. Write down responses to all of the questions in the inventory; then think through all of these potential topic areas before making a decision about your topic.

Once you have determined your topic, begin to plan your speech. Be certain that it has an introduction, body, and conclusion. Start by planning the body of your speech. In the body you will develop your major ideas (main points). You may include up to three main points in your presentation. Each main point must be supported by facts and figures, examples, or narratives. These materials should be inserted into the outline worksheet in the appropriate places.

After you have prepared the body of your speech, you should develop an introduction that grabs the audience's attention and leads into the body of your speech. Finally, you should prepare a conclusion that summarizes your message and concluding remarks that reflect on the meaning and significance of your speech.

Copyright © Houghton Mifflin Company. All rights reserved.

Self-awareness Inventory

1. What factors in my cultural background have influenced me the most? _____

_____

_____

_____

_____

2. What factors in my environment have influenced me the most? _____

_____

_____

_____

_____

3. What person or persons have had a real impact on my life? _____

_____

_____

_____

_____

4. What experiences have I had that have shaped me as a person? _____

_____

_____

_____

Copyright © Houghton Mifflin Company. All rights reserved.

5. What activities of mine define me as a person? _____

    _____

    _____

    _____

    _____

6. What type of influence has my work had in shaping me? _____

    _____

    _____

    _____

    _____

7. Do I have a goal or purpose in life that shapes my behavior? _____

    _____

    _____

    _____

    _____

8. Do I have special values that influence my life? _____

    _____

    _____

    _____

    _____

Copyright © Houghton Mifflin Company. All rights reserved.

Outline Format for a Self-introductory Speech

Introduction

I. Attention-arousing and orienting material: _____

_____

_____

_____

II. Preview: _____

_____

_____

Body

I. Main point #1: _____

_____

Supporting material: _____

_____

_____

_____

II. Main point #2: _____

_____

Supporting material: _____

_____

_____

_____

Copyright © Houghton Mifflin Company. All rights reserved.

III. Main point #3: _____

_____

Supporting material: _____

_____

_____

_____

Conclusion

I. Summary statement: _____

_____

_____

II. Concluding remarks: _____

_____

_____

_____

_____

Copyright © Houghton Mifflin Company. All rights reserved.

Checklist for a Self-introductory Speech

_____   I have narrowed my topic to one thing that best defines me as an individual.

_____   My introduction creates attention and interest.

_____   My introduction previews the main point(s) of my speech.

_____   The body of my speech contains one, two, or three main points.

_____   Each main point of my speech is supported by either facts and figures, examples, or narratives.

_____   My conclusion contains a summary that restates my message.

_____   I end my speech with concluding remarks that leave the audience with something to remember.

Copyright © Houghton Mifflin Company. All rights reserved.

Practice Presentation Feedback Form

1. Did the introduction gain your attention? What other techniques might the speaker want to consider?

2. Did the introduction adequately preview the speech? Would such a preview be desirable or necessary?

3. Was the purpose of the speech clear? What was it?

4. Could you detect the main points of the speech? What were they?

5. Was there sufficient supporting material? Were the examples or narratives interesting?

6. Did the conclusion effectively summarize the message?

7. Did the concluding remarks leave you with something to remember?

8. Did the presentation sound natural and spontaneous?

9. What specific advice would you offer the speaker for his or her next presentation?

Copyright © Houghton Mifflin Company. All rights reserved.

Evaluation Form for a Self-introductory Speech

Name: _____ Date: _____ Topic: _____

General

_____ Did the speaker seem committed to the topic?

_____ Did the speech fulfill the specifics of the assignment?

_____ Did the speech promote identification among topic, audience, and speaker?

_____ Was purpose of the speech clear?

_____ Was the topic handled with imagination and freshness?

_____ Did the speech meet high ethical standards?

Substance and Structure

_____ Did the introduction arouse your interest?

_____ Was the speech easy to follow?

_____ Could you identify the main points of the speech?

_____ Were main ideas supported by examples or narratives?

_____ Did the conclusion help you remember the speech?

Presentation

_____ Was the language clear, simple, and direct?

_____ Was the language colorful?

_____ Were the grammar and pronunciations correct?

_____ Was the speech presented extemporaneously?

_____ Were notes used unobtrusively?

_____ Was the speech presented enthusiastically?

_____ Did the speaker maintain good eye contact?

_____ Did the presentation sound "conversational"?

Comments:

Grade _____

Copyright © Houghton Mifflin Company. All rights reserved

Personal Report of Communication Apprehension Scale*

Directions: This instrument is composed of 20 statements concerning your feelings about communication with other people. Please indicate in the space provided the degree to which each statement applies to you by marking whether you

> 1 = strongly agree
> 2 = agree
> 3 = are undecided
> 4 = disagree
> 5 = strongly disagree

There are no right or wrong answers. Many of the statements are similar to other statements. Do not be concerned about this. Work quickly—just record your first impressions.

_____ 1. When participating in a meeting with people I don't know well, I feel very nervous.

_____ 2. I have no fear of facing an audience.

_____ 3. I look forward to expressing my opinions at meetings.

_____ 4. I look forward to having an opportunity to speak in public.

_____ 5. I find the prospect of speaking somewhat pleasant.

_____ 6. When I am speaking in public, my posture feels strained and unnatural.

_____ 7. I am tense and nervous while participating in group discussions.

_____ 8. Although I talk fluently with friends, I am at a loss for words before an audience.

_____ 9. My hands tremble when I try to handle objects during a presentation.

_____ 10. I always avoid speaking in public if possible.

_____ 11. I feel that I am more fluent when talking in meetings than most other people are.

_____ 12. I am fearful and tense all the while I am speaking before a group of people.

_____ 13. My thoughts become confused and jumbled when I speak before an audience.

_____ 14. Although I am nervous just before getting up to speak, I soon forget my fears and enjoy the experience.

_____ 15. Talking to people who hold positions of authority makes me fearful and tense.

_____ 16. I dislike using my voice and body expressively.

_____ 17. I feel relaxed and comfortable while speaking.

_____ 18. I feel self-conscious when I am called upon to answer a question or give an opinion in class.

_____ 19. I face the prospect of making a speech with complete confidence.

_____ 20. I would enjoy presenting a speech on a local television show.

---

* Adapted from James C. McCroskey, *An Introduction to Rhetorical Communication,* 6th ed. (Englewood Cliffs, NJ: Prentice-Hall) 1993, pp. 37–39.

Copyright © Houghton Mifflin Company. All rights reserved.

Scoring the Personal Report of Communication Apprehension Scale

Scoring

(1) Add the responses to the following questions to obtain the N: score:

$$N = 1 + 6 + 7 + 8 + 9 + 10 + 12 + 13 + 15 + 16 + 18$$

(2) Add the responses to the following questions to obtain the P: score:

$$P = 2 + 3 + 4 + 5 + 11 + 14 + 17 + 19 + 20$$

(3) Substitute the N and P scores in the following formula to determine your total score:

$$CA = (66 - N) + P$$

Descriptive Statistics

Range:	20–100
Mean:	50.45
Standard deviation:	11.58
Internal reliability:	.93
Excessive apprehension:	62 and higher

Copyright © Houghton Mifflin Company. All rights reserved.

Listening Problems Checklist

_____ 1. I believe listening is an automatic process, not a learned behavior.

_____ 2. I stop listening and think about something else when a speech is uninteresting.

_____ 3. I find it hard to listen to speeches on topics about which I feel strongly.

_____ 4. I react emotionally to trigger words.

_____ 5. I am easily distracted by noises when someone is speaking.

_____ 6. I don't like to listen to speakers who are not experts.

_____ 7. I find some people too objectionable to listen to.

_____ 8. I nod off when someone speaks in a monotone.

_____ 9. I can be so dazzled by a glib presentation that I don't really listen to the speaker.

_____ 10. I don't like to listen to speeches that contradict my values.

_____ 11. I think up counterarguments when I disagree with a speaker's perspective.

_____ 12. I know so much about some topics that I can't learn from most speakers.

_____ 13. I believe the speaker is the one responsible for effective communication.

_____ 14. I find it hard to listen when I have a lot on my mind.

_____ 15. I stop listening when a subject is difficult to understand.

_____ 16. I can look like I'm listening when I am not.

_____ 17. I listen only for facts and ignore the rest of a message.

_____ 18. I try to write down everything a lecturer says.

_____ 19. I let a speaker's appearance determine how well I will listen.

_____ 20. I often jump to conclusions before I have listened all the way through a message.

Copyright © Houghton Mifflin Company. All rights reserved.

Speech Evaluation Form

Speaker: _____ Topic: _____ Date: _____

Overall Considerations

_____ Did the speaker seem committed to the topic?
_____ Did the speech meet the requirements of the assignment?
_____ Was the speech adapted to fit the audience?
_____ Did the speech promote identification among topic, audience, and speaker?
_____ Was the purpose of the speech clear?
_____ Was the topic handled with imagination and freshness?
_____ Did the speech meet high ethical standards?

Substance

_____ Was the topic worthwhile?
_____ Had the speaker done sufficient research?
_____ Were the main ideas supported with reliable and relevant information?
_____ Was testimony used appropriately?
_____ Were the sources documented appropriately?
_____ Were examples or narratives used effectively?
_____ Was the reasoning clear and correct?

Structure

_____ Did the introduction spark your interest?
_____ Did the introduction adequately preview the message?
_____ Was the speech easy to follow?
_____ Could you identify the main points of the speech?
_____ Were transitions used to tie the sections of the speech together?
_____ Did the conclusion summarize the message?
_____ Did the conclusion help you remember the speech?

Presentation

_____ Was the language clear, simple, and direct?
_____ Was the language colorful?
_____ Were the grammar and pronunciations correct?
_____ Was the speech presented extemporaneously?
_____ Were notes used unobtrusively?
_____ Was the speaker appropriately enthusiastic?
_____ Did the speaker maintain good eye contact?
_____ Did the speaker's gestures and body language complement the ideas?
_____ Was the speaker's voice expressive?
_____ Were the speaker's delivery rate and loudness appropriate to the material?
_____ Did the speaker use pauses appropriately?
_____ Did presentation aids make the message clearer or more memorable?
_____ Were presentation aids skillfully integrated into the speech?
_____ Was the presentation free from distracting mannerisms?

Copyright © Houghton Mifflin Company. All rights reserved.

Guidelines for Evaluating an Outside Speaker

1. How would you rate the speaker's ethos?

2. Was the speech well adapted to the audience's needs and interests?

3. Did the speech take into account the cultural complexity of its audience?

4. Was the speech attuned to audience values?

5. Was the message clear?

6. Was the message well structured?

7. Was language used effectively?

8. Was the speech skillfully presented?

9. How did the listeners respond, both during and after the speech?

10. Did the communication environment have an impact on the message?

11. Did the speech achieve its goals?

12. Was the speech ethical in terms of responsible knowledge and the use of communication techniques?

Copyright © Houghton Mifflin Company. All rights reserved.

Audience Analysis Questionnaire

Sex: M F   Age: _____   Academic year: FR SO JR SR   GPA: _____   Race: _____

Marital status: _____   Religious preference: _____

Major: _____   State lived in longest: _____

Current job (full- or part-time): _____   Hours per week: _____

Career aspirations: _____

Persons I admire most: (male) _____ (female) _____

Political preferences: liberal, conservative, moderate   Democrat, Republican, other
                                    (circle one)   (circle one)

Group memberships (occupational, political, religious, or social): _____

_____

_____

Father's occupation: _____   Mother's occupation: _____

Place of birth: _____   Places lived: _____

Travel (in USA): _____

Travel (outside USA): _____

Hobbies: _____

_____

Positive "trigger words": _____

Negative "trigger words": _____

The most important thing in my life right now is _____

_____

Topics on which I would like to hear an informative speech (name 3): _____

_____

Topics on which I would like to hear a persuasive speech (name 3): _____

_____

Copyright © Houghton Mifflin Company. All rights reserved.

College Student Attitude Questionnaire

Respond to each of the following statements by placing the number of the option that best represents your position in the space before the item. Do not put your name on this questionnaire. All responses should be anonymous and will be kept confidential.

5	=	I strongly agree with this statement.
4	=	I somewhat agree with this statement.
3	=	I have no opinion on this statement.
2	=	I disagree somewhat with this statement.
1	=	I strongly disagree with this statement.

_____ 1. I try to keep up with political affairs.

_____ 2. The government should do more to control the sale of handguns.

_____ 3. There is too much concern in the courts for the rights of criminals.

_____ 4. Better education and more job opportunities would substantially reduce crime.

_____ 5. The government is not doing enough to control pollution.

_____ 6. If two people really like each other, it's all right for them to have sex, even if they've only known each other for a very short time.

_____ 7. The activities of married women are best confined to the home and family.

_____ 8. Abortion should be legal.

_____ 9. It is important to have laws prohibiting homosexual relationships.

_____ 10. Wealthy people should pay a larger share of taxes than they do now.

_____ 11. Taxes should be raised to reduce the deficit.

_____ 12. Marijuana should be legalized.

_____ 13. Employers should be allowed to require drug testing of employees or job applicants.

_____ 14. Racial discrimination is no longer a major problem in America.

_____ 15. Affirmative action in college admissions should be abolished.

_____ 16. A national health care plan is needed to cover everybody's medical costs.

Thank you for your cooperation.

Copyright © Houghton Mifflin Company. All rights reserved.

Assessing Your Speech Environment

1. Should you anticipate any problems with your presentations due to time or timing?

2. What should you consider about the physical setting in which you will be speaking? How might the size of the room or the availability of special equipment affect your presentation?

3. How might audience expectations for this particular occasion affect your presentation?

4. Is there any late-breaking news that might affect the way in which your audience perceives your topic?

5. Is there a good chance that other speakers might address your topic before you do? If so, how would you adjust to this situation?

6. How large and diverse is your audience? Who is your primary audience? How might this factor relate to your preparation and presentation?

Copyright © Houghton Mifflin Company. All rights reserved.

Assessing Your Audience

1. What beliefs, attitudes, needs, interests, or values do you share with the members of your primary audience? How might you build on this common ground to support your thesis?

2. What audience demographics (age, gender, education level, group and political affiliations, religion, sociocultural background) might be relevant to your topic and purpose/thesis statements? Can your audience be characterized according to predominant demographic characteristics?

3. How important is your topic to your audience? Do they already care about it? Why? If not, how can you motivate them to listen?

4. What aspects of your topic will be most relevant to them? How might you best gain and hold their attention from the beginning of your speech?

5. What do they already know about your topic? What do they want and need to know in order for you to establish your main points and assertions responsibly?

6. How do they feel about your topic? Would they be predisposed to act in a positive, neutral, or negative fashion? Can you think of any obvious reasons why they may not be open to your proposal or to any other new ideas represented by your topic and purpose?

Copyright © Houghton Mifflin Company. All rights reserved.

Values Survey I

On this page are eighteen values listed in alphabetical order. Your task is to arrange them in the order of their importance to YOU. Study the list carefully and pick out the one value which is most important to you. Write the letter of that value on the line next to number 1. Then pick out the value that is the second most important and write the letter of that value on the line next to number 2. Continue to do the same for each of the remaining values. The value which is the least important to you goes on the line next to number 18.

1. _____   A. A comfortable life

2. _____   B. An exciting life

3. _____   C. A sense of accomplishment

4. _____   D. A world at peace

5. _____   E. A world of beauty

6. _____   F. Equality

7. _____   G. Family security

8. _____   H. Freedom

9. _____   I. Happiness

10. _____   J. Inner harmony

11. _____   K. Mature love

12. _____   L. National security

13. _____   M. Pleasure

14. _____   N. Salvation

15. _____   O. Self-respect

16. _____   P. Social recognition

17. _____   Q. True friendship

18. _____   R. Wisdom

Copyright © Houghton Mifflin Company. All rights reserved.

Values Survey II

On this page are eighteen values listed in alphabetical order. Your task is to arrange them in the order of their importance to YOU. Study the list carefully and pick out the one value which is most important to you. Write the letter of that value on the line next to number 1. Then pick out the value that is the second most important and write the letter of that value on the line next to number 2. Continue to do the same for each of the remaining values. The value which is the least important to you goes on the line next to number 18.

1. _____	A.	Ambitious
2. _____	B.	Broadminded
3. _____	C.	Capable
4. _____	D.	Cheerful
5. _____	E.	Clean
6. _____	F.	Courageous
7. _____	G.	Forgiving
8. _____	H.	Helpful
9. _____	I.	Honest
10. _____	J.	Imaginative
11. _____	K.	Independent
12. _____	L.	Intellectual
13. _____	M.	Logical
14. _____	N.	Loving
15. _____	O.	Obedient
16. _____	P.	Polite
17. _____	Q.	Responsible
18. _____	R.	Self-controlled

Copyright © Houghton Mifflin Company. All rights reserved.

Revised Gene Scale

SA A N D SD   1. Most other cultures seem backward when compared to my culture.

SA A N D SD   2. People in other cultures have a better lifestyle than we do in my culture.

SA A N D SD   3. Most people would be happier if they didn't live as people do in my culture.

SA A N D SD   4. My culture should be the role model for other cultures.

SA A N D SD   5. Lifestyles in other cultures are just as valid as those in my culture.

SA A N D SD   6. Other cultures should try to be more like my culture.

SA A N D SD   7. I'm not interested in the values and customs of other cultures.

SA A N D SD   8. It is not wise for other cultures to look up to my culture.

SA A N D SD   9. People in my culture could learn a lot from people in other cultures.

SA A N D SD   10. Most people from other cultures just don't know what's good for them.

SA A N D SD   11. People from my culture act strangely and oddly when they go into other cultures.

SA A N D SD   12. I have little respect for the values and customs of other cultures.

SA A N D SD   13. Most people would be happier if they lived as people in my culture do.

SA A N D SD   14. People in my culture have just about the best lifestyles available anywhere.

SA A N D SD   15. My culture seems backward when compared to most other cultures.

SA A N D SD   16. My culture is a poor role model for other cultures.

SA A N D SD   17. Lifestyles in other cultures are not as valid as those in my culture.

SA A N D SD   18. My culture should try to be more like other cultures.

SA A N D SD   19. I'm very interested in the values and customs of other cultures.

SA A N D SD   20. Most people in my culture just don't know what's good for them.

SA A N D SD   21. People in other cultures could learn a lot from people in my culture.

SA A N D SD   22. Other cultures are wise to look up to my culture.

SA A N D SD   23. I respect the values and customs of other cultures.

SA A N D SD   24. People from other cultures act strangely and oddly when they come into my culture.

Copyright © Houghton Mifflin Company. All rights reserved.

Please Fill in the Blanks

1. After a hard day on the job, the secretary _____

   _____

2. When the plumber arrived at my house, _____

   _____

3. The doctor was most helpful with my problems; in fact, _____

   _____

4. My child's teacher is outstanding; for example, _____

   _____

5. When a basketball player graduates from college, _____

   _____

6. On the tour the president was accompanied by _____

   _____

7. While I was in the hospital, I had the most wonderful nurse. In fact, ____

   _____

8. When the construction supervisor arrived at the scene of the accident, ___

   _____

Copyright © Houghton Mifflin Company. All rights reserved.

Avoiding Sexist Language

What alternatives can you suggest for the following words?

Early man   _____

Mankind   _____

Mailman   _____

Man-made   _____

Congressman   _____

Chairman   _____

Repairman   _____

Businessman   _____

Manpower   _____

Copyright © Houghton Mifflin Company. All rights reserved.

Audience Analysis Worksheet

Topic: _____

Audience: _____

Factor description   **Adaptations needed**

Time: _____   _____

Place: _____   _____

Occasion: _____   _____

Audience size: _____   _____

Context: _____   _____

Age: _____   _____

Gender: _____   _____

Education level: _____   _____

_____   _____

Group affiliations: _____   _____

_____   _____

Sociocultural background: _____   _____

_____   _____

Interest in topic: _____   _____

_____   _____

_____   _____

Knowledge of topic: _____   _____

_____   _____

_____   _____

Attitude regarding topic: _____   _____

_____   _____

_____   _____

Values regarding topic: _____   _____

_____   _____

_____   _____

Motivational appeals: _____   _____

_____   _____

_____   _____

Copyright © Houghton Mifflin Company. All rights reserved.

Source Credibility Questionnaire

Students use a variety of sources when preparing classroom speeches. These sources may range from highly credible to barely believable. A highly credible source is one that is seen as **accurate, unbiased, trustworthy,** and **fair.**

The following is a list of sources frequently used in student speeches. Please use the following scale to indicate how credible you believe each source is:

        5 = very high credibility
        4 = high credibility
        3 = average credibility
        2 = low credibility
        1 = very low credibility
        N = not familiar with this publication

Please circle the appropriate number that represents your estimation of the credibility of each of the following publications:

Time Magazine	5	4	3	2	1	N
Cosmopolitan	5	4	3	2	1	N
Changing Times	5	4	3	2	1	N
The New Yorker	5	4	3	2	1	N
Esquire	5	4	3	2	1	N
Today's Health (AMA)	5	4	3	2	1	N
Wall Street Journal	5	4	3	2	1	N
National Geographic	5	4	3	2	1	N
Reader's Digest	5	4	3	2	1	N
U.S. News and World Report	5	4	3	2	1	N
Sports Illustrated	5	4	3	2	1	N
Ladies' Home Journal	5	4	3	2	1	N
New England Journal of Medicine	5	4	3	2	1	N
National Inquirer	5	4	3	2	1	N
New York Times	5	4	3	2	1	N
People	5	4	3	2	1	N
Playboy	5	4	3	2	1	N
Newsweek	5	4	3	2	1	N
Psychology Today	5	4	3	2	1	N
Ms.	5	4	3	2	1	N
TV Guide	5	4	3	2	1	N
Harvard Business Review	5	4	3	2	1	N
Field and Stream	5	4	3	2	1	N
Ebony	5	4	3	2	1	N
Popular Mechanics	5	4	3	2	1	N
The American Psychologist	5	4	3	2	1	N
Money	5	4	3	2	1	N
Rolling Stone	5	4	3	2	1	N
USA Today	5	4	3	2	1	N

Age: _____ Sex: _____ Race: _____ Classification: Sr   Jr   Soph   Fresh   Other

Copyright © Houghton Mifflin Company. All rights reserved.

Personal Interest Inventory

Places

_____

_____

_____

_____

_____

_____

People

_____

_____

_____

_____

_____

_____

Activities

_____

_____

_____

_____

_____

_____

Objects

_____

_____

_____

_____

_____

_____

Events

_____

_____

_____

_____

_____

_____

Goals

_____

_____

_____

_____

_____

_____

Values

_____

_____

_____

_____

_____

_____

Problems

_____

_____

_____

_____

_____

_____

Campus Concerns

_____

_____

_____

_____

_____

_____

Copyright © Houghton Mifflin Company. All rights reserved.

Audience Interest Inventory

Places

_____

_____

_____

_____

_____

_____

People

_____

_____

_____

_____

_____

_____

Activities

_____

_____

_____

_____

_____

_____

Objects

_____

_____

_____

_____

_____

_____

Events

_____

_____

_____

_____

_____

_____

Goals

_____

_____

_____

_____

_____

_____

Values

_____

_____

_____

_____

_____

Problems

_____

_____

_____

_____

_____

Campus Concerns

_____

_____

_____

_____

_____

Copyright © Houghton Mifflin Company. All rights reserved.

Personal and Audience Interests Worksheet

Personal Interests	Audience Interests	Potential Topics
_____	_____	_____
_____	_____	_____
_____	_____	_____
_____	_____	_____
_____	_____	_____
_____	_____	_____

Copyright © Houghton Mifflin Company. All rights reserved.

Topic Focusing Worksheet

Who: _____

_____

_____

What: _____

_____

_____

When: _____

_____

_____

Where: _____

_____

_____

Why: _____

_____

_____

How: _____

_____

_____

Copyright © Houghton Mifflin Company. All rights reserved.

Personal Knowledge and Experience Worksheet

What I know: **Where/how I learned it:**   **What I need to find out:**

_____   _____   _____

_____   _____   _____

_____   _____   _____

_____   _____   _____

_____   _____   _____

_____   _____   _____

Examples/narratives I might use:

_____

_____

_____

_____

_____

_____

Copyright © Houghton Mifflin Company. All rights reserved.

Research Strategy Worksheet

TOPIC: _____

SPECIFIC PURPOSE: _____

GENERAL INFORMATION SOURCE (List a source of general information applicable to your topic):

_____

KEY TERMS AND ACCESS TO INFORMATION SOURCES (List the key terms you will use and two sources of access to information you will use to identify specific and/or in-depth references):

Key Terms: 1. _____   2. _____

Access: 1. _____   2. _____

SPECIFIC AND/OR IN-DEPTH INFORMATION REFERENCES (List three or four references to specific and/or in-depth information applicable to your topic. At least two must be from periodicals or books):

1. _____

_____

2. _____

_____

3. _____

_____

4. _____

_____

CURRENT INFORMATION REFERENCES (List one or two sources of current information if they are applicable to your topic):

1. _____

_____

2. _____

_____

LOCAL APPLICATIONS SOURCES (List one or two sources for local applications material if they relate to your topic):

1. _____

_____

2. _____

_____

Copyright © Houghton Mifflin Company. All rights reserved.

Research Overview Form
(Page 1)

Source:

_____

_____

_____

Main Points:

_____

_____

_____

_____

Source:

_____

_____

Main Points:

_____

_____

_____

_____

Source:

_____

_____

Main Points:

_____

_____

_____

_____

Copyright © Houghton Mifflin Company. All rights reserved.

Research Overview Form
(Page 2)

Source:

_____

_____

_____

Main Points:

_____

_____

_____

_____

Source:

_____

_____

_____

Main Points:

_____

_____

_____

_____

Source:

_____

_____

_____

Main Points:

_____

_____

_____

_____

Copyright © Houghton Mifflin Company. All rights reserved.

Guidelines for Supporting a Point

This is an exercise to help you learn how to use supporting materials effectively in your speeches. It provides you with an opportunity to make a relatively simple presentation to your audience. The research that you need to do for this presentation and the time that it should take you to organize and prepare it are minimal.

Begin by deciding on a statement, claim, or assertion that would need to be supported before listeners would accept it. Write this in the proper place on your outline worksheet. Next, go to the library to research the statement you wish to support. Look for facts and information that support your statement. Facts are verifiable units of information and should come from sources which the audience respects. Your information should be relevant to your claim and should contain the most recent facts on the topic. Put this information in the designated place on your outline worksheet. After you have entered your factual information, find some testimony that supports your statement and include it in the appropriate space on the worksheet. You should use expert testimony from a source who is competent to speak on the subject. Next, find an example or narrative that further demonstrates your point. Enter this material in the appropriate space on the worksheet.

Once you have decided on the facts and figures, testimony, and narrative examples you will use to support your point, you should plan transitions so that your presentation flows smoothly. You should have transitions between the statement and supporting materials, between the different types of supporting materials, and between the supporting materials and the restatement of your original assertion. Prepare these transitions and insert them into the worksheet in the appropriate places.

Copyright © Houghton Mifflin Company. All rights reserved.

Outline Worksheet for Supporting a Point

Statement: _____

Transition into facts or statistics: _____

_____

    1. Factual information or statistics to support statement: _____

_____

_____

_____

Transition into testimony: _____

_____

    2. Testimony to support statement: _____

_____

_____

_____

Transition into example or narrative: _____

_____

    3. Example or narrative to support statement: _____

_____

_____

_____

Transition into restatement: _____

_____

Restatement: _____

Works Cited:

Copyright © Houghton Mifflin Company. All rights reserved.

Checklist for Supporting a Point

_____ I have selected a claim or assertion that needs to be supported before it can be accepted by my audience.

_____ I have selected facts and figures from a credible, unbiased source of information.

_____ I have identified the source(s) of my information.

_____ I have found expert testimony to support my claim or assertion.

_____ I have introduced the source of the testimony and have established his or her credentials to speak on the topic.

_____ I have developed an example or narrative that focuses attention on the most important aspect of my claim or assertion.

_____ I have planned transitions to make my presentation flow smoothly.

_____ I have prepared a list of works consulted that contains at least two references, only one of which is from an encyclopedia or dictionary.

Copyright © Houghton Mifflin Company. All rights reserved.

Evaluation of a One-Point Presentation

NAME: _____   SECTION: _____   GRADE: _____

Factual information or statistics:

Relevance to point	5	4	3	2	1
Recency of information/statistics	5	4	3	2	1
Source/date identified	5	4	3	2	1
Credibility of source	5	4	3	2	1
Freedom from distortion	5	4	3	2	1
Facts rather than opinions	5	4	3	2	1

Testimony:

Relevance to point	5	4	3	2	1
Recency of testimony	5	4	3	2	1
Proper type of testimony used	5	4	3	2	1
Qualifications specified	5	4	3	2	1
Accuracy of quote or paraphrase	5	4	3	2	1

Example or narrative:

Relevance to point	5	4	3	2	1
Representative of situation	5	4	3	2	1
Plausibility	5	4	3	2	1
Interest value	5	4	3	2	1

General:

Use of transitions to integrate	5	4	3	2	1
Extemporaneous presentation	5	4	3	2	1

Comments:

Copyright © Houghton Mifflin Company. All rights reserved.

Possible Topics for Stories

The most exciting day of my life

The worst day of my life

How I met the person I am dating/married to

A story my mother/father told me

A story I want to tell my children

A story that reflects my cultural background

The scariest dream I ever had

The wildest dream I ever had

The sweetest dream I ever had

How I learned how to laugh at myself

How I learned the importance of telling the truth

How I bought my first _____

How I got taken for a sucker

The story of my bravest hour

How I decided on my major

The funniest thing my pet ever did

The funniest thing a member of my family ever did

The funniest thing I ever did

The dumbest thing I ever did

The smartest thing I ever did

How I overcame a problem with _____

The nicest thing anyone ever did for me

The meanest thing anyone ever did to me

Copyright © Houghton Mifflin Company. All rights reserved.

Worksheet for Structural Analysis

Introduction

Attention material: _____

Establishment of ethos: _____

Preview or transition: _____

Length (in relation to body and conclusion): _____

Body

Main point #1: _____

    Type and amount of support: _____

    Transition to point #2: _____

    Length (relative to other main points): _____

Main point #2: _____

    Type and amount of support: _____

    Transition to point #3: _____

    Length (relative to other main points): _____

Main point #3: _____

    Type and amount of support: _____

    Transition to conclusion: _____

    Length (relative to other main points): _____

Conclusion

Summary of message: _____

Concluding material: _____

Length (in relation to body and introduction): _____

Copyright © Houghton Mifflin Company. All rights reserved.

Structuring Worksheet
(Page 1)

Name: _____   Topic: _____

Time—a series of events or steps in a process; events or steps must follow a specific order.
Residual Message: When I am done with my speech, I want my audience to know that

_____

_____

_____

_____

Space—parts of something and how they fit together to form the whole either literally or figuratively
Residual Message: When I am done with my speech, I want my audience to know that

_____

_____

_____

_____

Classification—Information-giving is the speaker's primary goal; categories must be comprised of relatively equal, non-overlapping main points.
Residual Message: When I am done with my speech, I want my audience to know that

_____

_____

_____

_____

Comparison—comparing things by showing their similarities
Residual Message: When I am done with my speech, I want my audience to know that

_____

_____

_____

_____

Copyright © Houghton Mifflin Company. All rights reserved.

Structuring Worksheet
(Page 2)

Contrast—comparing things by showing their differences

Residual Message: When I am done with my speech, I want my audience to know that

_____

_____

_____

_____

Cause-Effect—the speaker establishes a relationship between two events or maintains that a certain result(s) is the product of a certain event(s).

Residual Message: When I am done with my speech, I want my audience to know that

Cause(s):   Effect(s):

_____   _____

_____   _____

_____   _____

Problem Solution—The speaker outlines a problem(s), offers a feasible solution(s), and illustrates the advantages of the solution or tells how the solution solves the problem.

Residual Message: When I am done with my speech I want my audience to know that

Problem: Solution: Advantage:

_____   _____   _____

_____   _____   _____

_____   _____   _____

Copyright © Houghton Mifflin Company. All rights reserved.

Checklist for Using Presentation Aids

_____ Will my presentation aid enhance understanding?

_____ Is my presentation aid easy to understand?

_____ Is there enough information on my presentation aid?

_____ Is there too much information on my presentation aid?

_____ Is my presentation aid neat?

_____ Is the print on my presentation aid large enough for all audience members to read?

_____ Is everything on my presentation aid drawn to scale?

_____ Do I have the necessary equipment to use my presentation aid?

_____ Do I know how to use the equipment?

_____ Will I need tape or thumbtacks to position my presentation aid?

_____ Have I practiced presenting my speech using my presentation aid?

_____ Could I give my speech just as well, if not better, without my presentation aid?

Copyright © Houghton Mifflin Company. All rights reserved.

How Much Is?

some? _____

a lot? _____

a little? _____

a whole lot? _____

scads? _____

a trifle? _____

just a tad? _____

many? _____

a good many? _____

several? _____

not many? _____

Copyright © Houghton Mifflin Company. All rights reserved.

New Adages for Old

Where there's a will, _____

Don't put all of your eggs _____

Where there's smoke, _____

Time and tide _____

Don't put the cart _____

A rolling stone _____

A bird in the hand _____

A stitch in time _____

He/she who hesitates _____

Look before you _____

Copyright © Houghton Mifflin Company. All rights reserved.

Guide for Evaluating a Presentation

1. Name, title, and/or position of speaker:

2. Subject, date, and time of speech:

3. Occasion for speech, including sponsoring group:

4. Location and physical setting of speech.

5. Mode of presentation (impromptu, memorized, manuscript, extemporaneous):

6. Discussion of appropriateness and effectiveness of mode of presentation:

7. Description and discussion of speaker's voice:

8. Discussion of appropriateness and effectiveness of rate of speaking (including the use of pauses):

9. Discussion of appropriateness and effectiveness of loudness (including any problems with equipment such as microphone squeal):

10. Discussion of speaker's vocal variety:

11. Discussion of speaker's articulation, enunciation, pronunciation, or dialect:

12. Discussion of speaker's use of body language (including facial expressions, eye contact, movement, gestures, and appearance):

13. Suggestions you would give this speaker for improving his or her presentation skills:

Copyright © Houghton Mifflin Company. All rights reserved.

Guide for Evaluating Voice and Articulation

Speaker's name: _____   Evaluated by: _____

1. What did you feel was the most effective aspect of the speaker's voice and articulation?

    _____

    _____

2. What did you feel was the least effective aspect of the speaker's voice and articulation?

    _____

    _____

3. Should the speaker try to raise or lower his/her habitual pitch? _____

4. Does the speaker tend to speak too rapidly or too slowly? _____

5. Does the speaker use pauses effectively? _____

6. Does the speaker speak too quietly or too loudly? _____

7. Does the speaker use enough vocal variety? _____

8. Does the speaker use acceptable articulation and enunciation? _____

9. Were any words mispronounced? _____

10. Is the speaker's dialect acceptable? _____

11. What recommendations would you make for the speaker's improvement? _____

    _____

Copyright © Houghton Mifflin Company. All rights reserved.

Guide for Evaluating Impromptu Presentations

Speaker: _____   Topic: _____   Date: _____

5 = excellent   4 = good   3 = average   2 = below average   1 = poor

Speaker opened with an introduction.	5	4	3	2	1
Main ideas were previewed.	5	4	3	2	1
Main ideas were easily identified.	5	4	3	2	1
Main ideas were adapted to audience.	5	4	3	2	1
Main ideas were properly supported.	5	4	3	2	1
Main ideas were easy to follow.	5	4	3	2	1
Main ideas were summarized.	5	4	3	2	1
Concluding remarks reflected on meaning.	5	4	3	2	1
Speaker maintained good eye contact.	5	4	3	2	1
Gestures were used effectively.	5	4	3	2	1
Rate of speaking was appropriate.	5	4	3	2	1
Loudness level was appropriate.	5	4	3	2	1
Vocal variety was appropriate.	5	4	3	2	1

Comments: _____

_____

_____

_____

_____

Grade: _____

Copyright © Houghton Mifflin Company. All rights reserved.

Evaluation Form for Question-and-Answer Sessions

Speaker: _____ Topic: _____ Date: _____

5 = excellent   4 = good   3 = average   2 = below average   1 = poor   NA = not applicable

Actively encouraged questions	5	4	3	2	1	NA
Well prepared to answer questions	5	4	3	2	1	NA
Repeated or paraphrased questions	5	4	3	2	1	NA
Maintained eye contact with audience	5	4	3	2	1	NA
Answers short and to the point	5	4	3	2	1	NA
Defused loaded questions	5	4	3	2	1	NA
Handled nonquestions appropriately	5	4	3	2	1	NA
Maintained control	5	4	3	2	1	NA
Observed time limits	5	4	3	2	1	NA
Concluded by refocusing on main points of prepared message	5	4	3	2	1	NA

Comments: _____

_____

_____

_____

_____

Grade: _____

Copyright © Houghton Mifflin Company. All rights reserved.

Evaluation Form for Televised Presentations

Speaker: _____ Topic: _____ Date: _____

5 = excellent   4 = good   3 = average   2 = below average   1 = poor   NA = not applicable

Speech appropriately timed	5	4	3	2	1	NA
Manuscript written in good oral style	5	4	3	2	1	NA
Colorful, memorable language	5	4	3	2	1	NA
Point, reason/example, restatement	5	4	3	2	1	NA
Sufficient previews and summaries	5	4	3	2	1	NA
Neat, well-groomed appearance	5	4	3	2	1	NA
Appropriate attire	5	4	3	2	1	NA
Good posture	5	4	3	2	1	NA
Conversational presentation	5	4	3	2	1	NA
Good use of vocal variety	5	4	3	2	1	NA
Eye contact through camera	5	4	3	2	1	NA
Gestures appropriately restrained	5	4	3	2	1	NA
Maintained demeanor through fade-out	5	4	3	2	1	NA

Comments: _____

_____

_____

_____

_____

Grade: _____

Copyright © Houghton Mifflin Company. All rights reserved.

Humor Orientation Scale*

Please respond to the following statements in terms of how well they describe your typical behavior. Use the following scale of agreement.

5 = strongly agree
4 = agree
3 = neutral
2 = disagree
1 = strongly disagree

_____ 1. I regularly tell jokes or funny stories when I am with a group.

_____ 2. People usually laugh when I tell a joke or story.

_____ 3. I have no memory for jokes or funny stories.

_____ 4. I can be funny without having to rehearse a joke.

_____ 5. Being funny is a natural communication style of mine.

_____ 6. I cannot tell a joke well.

_____ 7. People seldom ask me to tell stories.

_____ 8. My friends would say that I am a funny person.

_____ 9. People don't seem to pay close attention when I tell a joke.

_____ 10. Even funny jokes seem flat when I tell them.

_____ 11. I can easily remember jokes and stories.

_____ 12. People often ask me to tell jokes and stories.

_____ 13. My friends would not say that I am a funny person.

_____ 14. I don't tell jokes or stories, even when asked to.

_____ 15. I tell stories and jokes very well.

_____ 16. Of all the people I know, I'm one of the funniest.

_____ 17. I use humor to communicate in a variety of situations.

---

*Adapted from Steve Booth-Butterfield and Melanie Booth-Butterfield, "Individual Differences in the Communication of Humorous Messages," *SSCJ*, Spring 1991, 32–40.

Copyright © Houghton Mifflin Company. All rights reserved.

Group Discussion Participant Evaluation Form

Person being evaluated: _____

Your name: _____ Date: _____

Use the following scale to describe the person assigned to you. Indicate your evaluation by circling one of the numbers to the left of each statement. You *must* describe and evaluate this student's performance.

1 = poor 2 = below average 3 = average 4 = above average 5 = superior

1	2	3	4	5	Appeared committed to the goals of the group
1	2	3	4	5	Participated frequently in group deliberations
1	2	3	4	5	Contributions were clear, relevant, and helpful.
1	2	3	4	5	Performed task leadership functions
1	2	3	4	5	Performed social leadership functions
1	2	3	4	5	Helped resolve conflict within the group
1	2	3	4	5	Encouraged participation of other group members
1	2	3	4	5	Helped keep the discussion focused on the problem
1	2	3	4	5	Contribution compared with that of other group members
1	2	3	4	5	Emerged as the leader of this group

Copyright © Houghton Mifflin Company. All rights reserved.

Leadership Potential Questionnaire

Leadership is composed of many facets. The ability to establish confidence, respect, and good rapport is required. Many people are afraid of assuming a leadership role. Others grow into it, although at first they might feel that they are not qualified. What about you?

This quiz is designed to help you measure your leadership potential by thinking back on real situations in your life and projecting yourself into possible future circumstances in which leadership might be required. Its purpose is to start you *thinking about* your leadership potential. It is not a scientifically developed measuring instrument. Respond as honestly as you can to the following items and see what you can learn about your leadership potential.

1. Your instructions were not followed and everything got messed up. Why?
    A. You did not foresee all the blunders your subordinates could make.
    B. It seems impossible to get halfway intelligent people to work these days.
    C. You did not explain the assignment in sufficient detail.

2. You have been asked to organize a group to improve your neighborhood. How would you react?
    A. Use an excuse, such as being too busy to get out of it.
    B. Ask someone who had organized such a group before to help you.
    C. Feel flattered and accept the assignment, even though it's a first for you.

3. Someone higher up in your group gives you an order. What are you most likely to do?
    A. Question the order and possibly suggest an alternative.
    B. Discuss the pros and cons and finally agree.
    C. An order is an order, and I carry it through as best I can.

4. You read about the chaotic state of affairs in another country. Finally, a strong person takes over and puts everything in better working order. How do you react to this news?
    A. Is he/she a dictator? I don't know, and if so, so what?
    B. It was necessary to introduce strong measures. The people always have to be led; later on they can participate again in decisions.
    C. Had the people been properly informed, they would have taken the right measures themselves.

5. You read the following statement: "He was relentless. He drove himself and others. He did not rest until he had reached a goal." What is your reaction?
    A. I am just like him.
    B. He is an unhappy person. I prefer to enjoy myself.
    C. If he could relax in between, it's okay; otherwise, I pity him.

6. You read in a person's obituary that he never complimented anyone in his organization. He watched every little detail. Managers were fired at the slightest pretext. He was feared by everybody, but he created a successful company.
    A. That is a very heavy price to pay. Probably nobody really liked him.
    B. Sometimes that is the only way to lead. The end result is really the important thing.
    C. He might have been more successful if he had been more human and caring.

Adapted from Ernest Dichter, *Total Self-Knowledge* (New York: Stein & Day, 1976), pp. 211–214. Copyright © 1976 by Ernest Dichter. Originally published by Stein & Day, Inc. Reprinted with permission of Scarborough House/Publishers and the author.

Copyright © Houghton Mifflin Company. All rights reserved.

What Kind of Leader Are You?*

For each of the following questions, circle the answer that best applies to you.

Yes No   1. Do you enjoy "running the show"?

Yes No   2. Generally, do you think it's worth the time and effort to explain the reasons for a decision or policy before putting it into effect?

Yes No   3. Do you prefer the administrative end of your leadership job—planning, paperwork, and so on—to supervising or working directly with your subordinates?

Yes No   4. A stranger comes into your department, and you know he's the new employee hired by one of your assistants. On approaching him, would you first ask *his* name rather than introduce yourself?

Yes No   5. Do you keep your people up to date as a matter of course on developments affecting the group?

Yes No   6. Do you find that in giving assignments, you tend to state the goals and leave the methods to your subordinates?

Yes No   7. Do you think that it's good common sense for a leader to keep aloof from his or her people because in the long run familiarity breeds lessened respect?

Yes No   8. It's time to decide about a group outing. You've heard that the majority prefer to have it on Wednesday, but you're pretty sure Thursday would be better for all concerned. Would you put the question to a vote rather than make the decision yourself?

Yes No   9. If you had your way, would you make running your group a push-button affair with personal contacts and communications held to a minimum?

Yes No 10. Do you find it fairly easy to fire someone?

Yes No 11. Do you feel that the friendlier you are with your people, the better you'll be able to lead them?

Yes No 12. After considerable time, you figure out the answer to a work problem. You pass along the solution to an assistant, who pokes it full of holes. Will you be annoyed that the problem is still unresolved rather than angry with the assistant?

Yes No 13. Do you agree that one of the best ways to avoid problems of discipline is to provide adequate punishments for violations of rules?

Yes No 14. Your way of handling a situation is being criticized. Would you try to sell your viewpoint to your group rather than make it clear that as boss, your decisions are final?

---

* Adapted from *Mastery of Management* by Auren Uris (1968), by permission of the Berkeley Publishing Company. (1968).

Copyright © Houghton Mifflin Company. All rights reserved.

Yes No 15. Do you generally leave it up to your subordinates to contact you as far as informal, day-to-day communications are concerned?

Yes No 16. Do you feel that everyone in your group should have a certain amount of personal loyalty to you?

Yes No 17. Do you favor the practice of appointing committees to settle a problem rather than stepping in to make a decision yourself?

Yes No 18. Some experts say differences of opinion within a work group are healthy. Others feel that such differences indicate basic flaws in group unity. Do you agree with the first view?

Scoring and Interpretation

To calculate your score, circle the question numbers 1 through 18 to which you answered *yes*. Then compare your answers with the following groupings.

A. 1, 4, 7, 10, 13, 16
B. 2, 5, 8, 11, 14, 17
C. 3, 6, 9, 12, 15, 18

If most of your *yes* answers correspond with Group A, chances are you tend to be an autocratic leader. If your total *yes* answers were highest in Group B, you probably have a predisposition toward being a participative leader. If Group C is the one in which you had the greatest number of *yes* answers, you are probably inclined toward being a free-rein leader.

Copyright © Houghton Mifflin Company. All rights reserved.

What Kind of Follower Are You?*

For each of the following questions circle the answer that best applies to you.

Yes No 1. When given an assignment, do you like to have all the details spelled out?

Yes No 2. Do you think that by and large most bosses are "bossier" than they need to be?

Yes No 3. Is initiative one of your stronger points?

Yes No 4. Do you feel that a boss lowers himself or herself by "palling around" with subordinates?

Yes No 5. In general, do you prefer working with others to working alone?

Yes No 6. Do you prefer the pleasures of solitude (reading, listening to music) to the social pleasures of being with others (parties, get-togethers, and so on)?

Yes No 7. Do you tend to become strongly attached to the boss you work for?

Yes No 8. Do you tend to offer a helping hand to the newcomers among your colleagues and coworkers?

Yes No 9. Do you enjoy using your own ideas and ingenuity to solve a work problem?

Yes No 10. Do you prefer the kind of boss who knows all the answers to one who comes to you for help?

Yes No 11. Do you feel it's okay for your boss to be friendlier with some members of the group than with others?

Yes No 12. Do you like to assume full responsibility for assignments rather than just to do the work and leave the responsibility to your boss?

Yes No 13. Do you feel that "mixed" groups—men working with women, for example—naturally tend to have more friction than unmixed ones?

Yes No 14. If you learned that your boss was having an affair with his or her secretary, would your respect for your boss remain undiminished?

Yes No 15. Have you always felt that "he travels fastest who travels alone"?

Yes No 16. Do you agree that a boss who couldn't win loyalty shouldn't be a boss?

Yes No 17. Would you be upset by a colleague whose inability or ineptitude obstructs the work of your department or company as a whole?

Yes No 18. Do you think *boss* is a dirty word?

---

* Adapted from *Mastery of Management* by Auren Uris (1968), by permission of the Berkeley Publishing Company. (1968).

Copyright © Houghton Mifflin Company. All rights reserved.

Scoring and Interpretation

To calculate your score, circle the question numbers 1 through 18 to which you answered *yes*. Then compare your answers with the following groupings.

  A. 1, 4, 7, 10, 13, 16
  B. 2, 5, 8, 11, 14, 17
  C. 3, 6, 9, 12, 15, 18

If most of your *yes* answers correspond with Group A, chances are you prefer autocratic leadership. If your total *yes* answers was highest in Group B, you probably prefer participative leadership. If Group C is one in which you had the most *yes* answers, you probably prefer free-rein leadership.

Copyright © Houghton Mifflin Company. All rights reserved.

What Design to Use When

Design	Use when
Spatial	Your topic can be discussed according to the way in which it is positioned in a physical setting or natural environment. This design allows you to take your audience on an orderly "oral tour" of your topic as you move from place to place.
Sequential	Your topic can be arranged in a time sequence. This design is useful for describing a process as a series of steps or for explaining a subject as a series of historical landmark developments. This design is also useful for presenting a plan of action in persuasive speeches.
Categorical	Your topic has natural or customary divisions. With this design, each category becomes a main point for development. It is useful when you need to organize large amounts of material. It is also useful in persuasive speeches to demonstrate that a plan will be *safe, inexpensive,* and *effective,* or to organize causes and consequences.
Comparative	Your topic is new to your audience, abstract, technical, or simply difficult to comprehend. This design helps to make material more meaningful by comparing or contrasting it with something the audience already knows and understands. It is useful in persuasive speeches when you want to demonstrate why your proposal is superior to another. It is especially good for speeches in which you contend with opposing views.
Causation	Your topic involves a situation, condition, or event that is best understood in terms of its underlying causes. This design may also be used to predict the future from existing conditions. It is useful in persuasive speeches for discussing the causes and consequences of a problem.
Problem-Solution	Your topic presents a problem that needs to be solved and a solution that will solve it. This design is good both for speeches involving attitudes and for speeches urging action.
Stock Issues	Your topic is one about which reasonable listeners might have questions that they would want answered before accepting your proposal.
Motivated Sequence	Your topic calls for action as the final phase of a five-step process that also involves (in this order) arousing attention, demonstrating need, satisfying need, picturing the results, and calling for action.
Refutative	You must answer strong opposition to a topic before you can establish your position. In this design, the major opposing claims become the main points for development. Contend with your weakest points first and avoid personal attacks.

Copyright © Houghton Mifflin Company. All rights reserved.

Guidelines for a Working Outline

A working outline helps you organize and develop your speech. It is a tentative plan that shows you how your ideas are evolving, whether they fit together, and if you have enough supporting materials.

This outline allows you to organize and reorganize your material as you work toward creating the formal outline of your speech. Use pencil so that you can make revisions without having to rewrite your entire working outline. You can use the worksheet on the following pages to rearrange your material as needed. In this way, you can refine the structure of your speech.

Start your working outline by listing your topic, specific purpose, and thesis statement. Keep these clearly in mind as you plan the body of your speech. Identify the main ideas (your main points) from your research. For each main point, determine the major subdivisions (subpoints) of the material. In later working outlines, you may also identify sub-sub points for each subpoint.

After you have identified your main points and subpoints, develop an introduction that fits the body of your speech. Your introduction should contain material that attracts attention, establishes your credibility, and previews your message. Next, you should prepare a conclusion that includes a summary and ending remarks. Finally, you should prepare transitions to use between the introduction and the body, between each of the main points, and between the body and the conclusion of your speech.

As you revise your working outline, be sure to also revise your preview and summary statements to reflect the changes you have made. As you save different versions of your working outline, you may wish to save them as "Working Outline 1, computers," "Working Outline 2, computers."

Copyright © Houghton Mifflin Company. All rights reserved.

Working Outline Worksheet

Title: _____

Topic: _____

Specific purpose: _____

_____

Thesis statement: _____

_____

Introduction

Attention material: _____

_____

_____

Credibility material: _____

_____

_____

Preview: _____

_____

_____

(Transition to body of speech)

_____

Body

Main point I: _____

_____

Subpoint A: _____

_____

_____

Copyright © Houghton Mifflin Company. All rights reserved.

Subpoint B: _____

_____

_____

(Transition to next main point)

_____

Main point II: _____

_____

Subpoint A: _____

_____

_____

Subpoint B: _____

_____

_____

(Transition to next main point)

_____

Main point III: _____

_____

Subpoint A: _____

_____

_____

Subpoint B: _____

_____

_____

Copyright © Houghton Mifflin Company. All rights reserved.

(Transition to next main point)

_____

Main point IV: _____

_____

    Subpoint A: _____

    _____

    _____

    Subpoint B: _____

    _____

    _____

(Transition to next main point)

_____

Main point V: _____

_____

    Subpoint A: _____

    _____

    _____

    Subpoint B: _____

    _____

    _____

(Transition to conclusion)

_____

Copyright © Houghton Mifflin Company. All rights reserved.

Conclusion

Summary: _____

_____

_____

Concluding remarks: _____

_____

_____

_____

Copyright © Houghton Mifflin Company. All rights reserved.

Checklist for a Working Outline

_____ 1. My topic, specific purpose, and thesis statement are clearly stated.

_____ 2. I have listed the most important ideas about my topic as main points.

_____ 3. I have no more than five main points.

_____ 4. Each subpoint breaks its main point into more specific detail.

_____ 5. My introduction contains attention-getting material, establishes my credibility, and previews my message.

_____ 6. I have prepared transitions to use between the introduction and the body, between each of the main points, and between the body and the conclusion of my speech.

_____ 7. I have revised my specific purpose, thesis statement, and preview as needed to reflect any changes in my working outline.

_____ 8. I have made several revisions of my working outline to be sure that my speech is well organized.

Copyright © Houghton Mifflin Company. All rights reserved.

Scrambled Outline I

Rearrange the elements of the following outline in a logical sequence.

Thesis statement: Deer hunting with a camera can be an exciting sport.

I. There is a profound quiet, a sense of mystery.
    A. The woods in the late fall are enchanting.
        1. The film-hunter becomes part of a beautiful scene.
        2. Dawn is especially lovely.
    B. Time that a big doe walked under my tree stand.
        1. When they appear, deer always surprise you.
        2. How a big buck surprised me after a long stalk.

II. Hunting from a stand can be a good way to capture a deer on film.
    A. Using the stalk method on the ground is another way to hunt with a camera.
        1. Learn to recognize deer tracks and droppings.
            a. Learn to recognize deer signs.
            b. Learn to recognize rubs on trees and scrapes on the ground.
        2. Hunt into the wind and move slowly.
    B. There are two main ways to hunt with a camera.
        1. Stands offer elevation above the line of sight.
        2. Portable stands are also available.
        3. Locating and building your permanent stand.

III. The right camera can be no more expensive than a rifle.
    A. Selecting the right camera for film-hunting is essential.
    B. Certain features—like a zoom lens—are necessary.

IV. Display slide of doe.
    A. You can collect "trophies" that you can enjoy forever.
    B. Display slide of buck.
    C. Not all hunters are killers: The film-hunter celebrates life, not death.

Copyright © Houghton Mifflin Company. All rights reserved.

Scrambled Outline II

Arrange the following elements into an outline.

1. There are existing organizations that students can support to help curb sexual assault rates.

2. Student crime-watch patrols could help curb sexual assault rates, theft, and assault at night.

3. Per capita rates of sexual assault are higher on campus than in many of our larger cities.

4. Today we've discussed the growing problem of crime on campus and what we, as students, can do about it.

5. Only you can lessen the chances that someday you or someone you love might become another victim.

6. As a victim of campus crime myself, I've become intimately concerned with this issue.

7. Only organized student involvement can help stem the tide of crime on campus.

8. We students should conduct a campaign against campus crime.

9. Last year seven cars and forty-two bicycles were stolen on campus.

10. Take Back the Night has been working for years to raise awareness about rape and its effects on women.

11. The problem of campus crime has been growing steadily for years.

12. Can anyone imagine being robbed or even raped at gunpoint in her own dorm building?

13. Student representatives could help pressure the administration to tighten campus security measures.

14. Rates of physical and violent assaults reported have increased 17 percent since 1990.

15. Today I'm going to talk to you about the growing problem of crime on campus and offer some solutions we can take to help curb it.

16. Men Against Rape needs volunteers to escort women on campus during evening hours.

17. Students could form a campuswide crime-watch program that works in cooperation with campus security.

18. To persuade my audience to conduct a campaign against campus crime

Copyright © Houghton Mifflin Company. All rights reserved.

Find the Fallacy

1. In 1931, approximately 6,000 workers were killed in industrial accidents in the United States. In 1945, over 9,000 workers were killed in industrial accidents. The rate of workers killed in industrial accidents rose dramatically between 1931 and 1945.

2. If we allow the communists a toehold in San Salvador, Mexico will be next.

3. Because the Great Depression began during Hoover's presidency, it is safe to assume that his economic policies were its primary cause.

4. Don't listen to environmentalists complain about acid rain. They're just a bunch of pot-smoking hippies.

5. My brother got a bad grade in algebra. My roommate got a bad grade in algebra. The girl sitting next to me in history class got a bad grade in algebra. Nobody makes a good grade in that class!

6. You know she can't be a good Republican. Her father was a liberal.

7. What's good for General Motors is good for America.

8. Salaries are really good at Gulf State Bank. They average more than $62,000 per year.

9. Don't tell me about recycling and the environment. By not being a vegetarian, you are ultimately contributing to environmental destruction yourself.

10. Everyone knows that taxes are bad for the economy.

Copyright © Houghton Mifflin Company. All rights reserved.

Informative Speech Evaluation Form

Name: _____ Date: _____ Topic: _____ Grade: _____

General

_____ Did the speaker seem committed to the topic?
_____ Did the speech fulfill the specifics of the assignment?
_____ Was the speech adapted to fit the audience?
_____ Did the speech promote identification among topic, audience, and speaker?
_____ Was the purpose of the speech clear?
_____ Was the topic handled with imagination and freshness?
_____ Did the speech meet high ethical standards?

Substance

_____ Was the topic worthwhile?
_____ Had the speaker done sufficient research?
_____ Were the main ideas supported with reliable information?
_____ Was testimony used appropriately?
_____ Were sources documented properly?
_____ Were examples and narratives used effectively?

Structure

_____ Did the introduction arouse interest?
_____ Did the introduction adequately preview the message?
_____ Was the speech easy to follow?
_____ Could you identify the main points of the speech?
_____ Were transitions used to tie the speech together?
_____ Did the conclusion help you remember the speech?

Presentation

_____ Was the language clear, simple, and direct?
_____ Was the language colorful?
_____ Were the grammar and pronunciations correct?
_____ Was the speech presented extemporaneously?
_____ Were notes used unobtrusively?
_____ Was the speech presented enthusiastically?
_____ Did the speaker maintain good eye contact?
_____ Did the presentation sound "conversational"?
_____ Did the gestures and body language complement ideas?
_____ Was the speaker's voice expressive?
_____ Were the rate and loudness appropriate to the material?
_____ Did the speaker use pauses appropriately?
_____ Did presentation aids make the message clearer or more memorable?
_____ Were presentation aids skillfully integrated into the speech?
_____ Was the presentation free from distracting mannerisms?

Comments:

Copyright © Houghton Mifflin Company. All rights reserved.

Persuasive Speech Evaluation Form

Name: _____ Date: _____ Topic: _____ Grade: _____

General

_____ Did the speaker seem committed to the topic?
_____ Did the speech fulfill the specifics of the assignment?
_____ Was the speech adapted to fit the audience?
_____ Did the speech promote identification among topic, audience, and speaker?
_____ Was purpose of the speech clear?
_____ Was the topic handled with imagination and freshness?
_____ Did the speech meet high ethical standards?

Substance

_____ Was the topic worthwhile?
_____ Had the speaker done sufficient research?
_____ Were the main ideas supported with reliable information?
_____ Was testimony used appropriately?
_____ Were sources documented properly?
_____ Were examples and narratives used effectively?
_____ Were appropriate proofs used?
_____ Was the reasoning clear?
_____ Did the reasoning follow an acceptable logical pattern?

Structure

_____ Did the introduction arouse interest?
_____ Did the introduction adequately preview the message?
_____ Was the speech easy to follow?
_____ Could you identify the main points of the speech?
_____ Were transitions used to tie the speech together?
_____ Did the conclusion help you remember the speech?

Presentation

_____ Was the language clear, simple, and direct?
_____ Was the language colorful?
_____ Were the grammar and pronunciations correct?
_____ Was the speech presented extemporaneously?
_____ Were notes used unobtrusively?
_____ Was the speech presented enthusiastically?
_____ Did the speaker maintain good eye contact?
_____ Did the presentation sound "conversational"?
_____ Did the gestures and body language complement ideas?
_____ Was the speaker's voice expressive?
_____ Were the rate and loudness appropriate to the material?
_____ Did the speaker use pauses appropriately?
_____ Did presentation aids make the message clearer or more memorable?
_____ Were presentation aids skillfully integrated into the speech?
_____ Was the presentation free from distracting mannerisms?

Comments:

Copyright © Houghton Mifflin Company. All rights reserved.

Ceremonial Speech Evaluation Form

Name: _____ Date: _____ Topic: _____ Grade: _____

General

_____ Did the speaker seem committed to the topic?
_____ Did the speech fulfill the specifics of the assignment?
_____ Did the speech promote identification among topic, audience, and speaker?
_____ Was purpose of the speech clear?
_____ Was the topic handled with imagination and freshness?

Substance

_____ Did the introduction arouse interest?
_____ Was the speech easy to follow?
_____ Could you identify the main points of the speech?
_____ Were the proper factors magnified in the presentation?
_____ Were the main ideas supported by examples or narratives?
_____ Did the conclusion help you remember the speech?

Presentation

_____ Was the language clear and direct?
_____ Was the language appropriate to the occasion?
_____ Were the grammar and pronunciations correct?
_____ Was the speech presented extemporaneously?
_____ Were notes used unobtrusively?
_____ Did the speaker maintain good eye contact?
_____ Did the presentation sound "conversational"?
_____ Did the gestures and body language complement ideas?
_____ Was the speaker's voice expressive?
_____ Were the rate and loudness appropriate to the material?
_____ Did the speaker use pauses appropriately?
_____ Was the presentation free from distracting mannerisms?

Comments:

Copyright © Houghton Mifflin Company. All rights reserved.

Self-evaluation Form

Name: _____   Date: _____

Topic: _____

Strengths of this assignment: _____

_____

_____

_____

_____

Areas that I need to work on: _____

_____

_____

_____

_____

Grade that I deserve: _____

* *

Instructor's evaluation:

Grade:

Copyright © Houghton Mifflin Company. All rights reserved.

Peer Evaluation Form

Speaker: _____   Topic: _____   Date: _____

Introduction:

1. Did the introduction gain your attention? How?
    _____
    _____

2. Did the speaker establish his or her credibility to speak on the topic? How?
    _____
    _____

3. Did the speaker adequately preview the main points?
    _____
    _____

Body:

1. Was the speech easy for you to follow? _____   Identify the main points:

    (1) _____
    (2) _____
    (3) _____

2. Were the main points arranged effectively? _____   What type of design was used?
    _____   Might a different design have been better? _____
    What design would you suggest? _____

3. Was the supporting material sufficient and appropriate? _____   Please comment:
    _____

4. Did you find the speech interesting? _____   Why or why not? _____
    _____

Conclusion:

1. Did the speaker summarize the message? _____
    _____

2. Did you feel that the speech was complete? _____
    _____

3. Were you left with something to remember? _____   What? _____
    _____

Suggestions for improvement (please note two things that the speaker could do to improve his/her next presentation):

1. _____
    _____

2. _____
    _____

Copyright © Houghton Mifflin Company. All rights reserved.

Guidelines for Using a Spatial Design

You should use a spatial design when your subject involves places or objects that can be put in a physical arrangement. This design takes your listeners on a systematic and orderly tour of your subject or systematically describes an arrangement so that your audience may visualize it accurately.

To develop the body of a speech using a spatial design, select a starting point and a direction of movement for the verbal journey on which you will take your listeners. Move in an orderly manner. Start a route and stay with it. Try not to backtrack or to jump from place to place. Your speech should build in interest as you move along to the last place, which should be the most interesting.

Copyright © Houghton Mifflin Company. All rights reserved.

Outline Worksheet: Spatial Design

Title (optional): _____

Topic: _____

Specific purpose: _____

_____

Thesis statement: _____

_____

Introduction

Attention material: _____

_____

Credibility material: _____

_____

Preview: _____

_____

(Transition to body of speech)

_____

Body

I. Main point #1 (Location 1): _____

_____

    A. (subpoint): _____

_____

    B. (subpoint): _____

_____

(Transition to Main point #2)

_____

Copyright © Houghton Mifflin Company. All rights reserved.

II. Main point #2 (Location 2): _____

_____

    A. (subpoint): _____

    _____

    B. (subpoint): _____

    _____

(Transition to Main point #3)

_____

III. Main point #3 (Location 3): _____

_____

    A. (subpoint) _____

    _____

    B. (subpoint) _____

    _____

(Transition to Main point #4)

_____

IV. Main point #4 (Location 4): _____

_____

    A. (subpoint): _____

    _____

    B. (subpoint): _____

    _____

(Transition to Main point #5)

_____

Copyright © Houghton Mifflin Company. All rights reserved.

V. Main point #5 (Location 5): _____

_____

    A. (subpoint): _____

    _____

    B. (subpoint): _____

    _____

(Transition to conclusion)

_____

Conclusion

    Summary: _____

    _____

    Concluding remarks: _____

    _____

Works Consulted:

Copyright © Houghton Mifflin Company. All rights reserved.

Checklist for a Spatial Design

_____ I have selected a topic that involves places or things that can be located physically.

_____ I have clearly stated the purpose of my speech.

_____ My thesis statement is written as a complete declarative sentence.

_____ My introduction gains attention and interest, establishes my credibility, and previews the main points of my message.

_____ My first main point is the starting point for the verbal journey of my speech.

_____ My speech moves from place to place in an orderly fashion.

_____ My speech builds interest as it moves from location to location.

_____ I have adequate supporting material for each main point in my speech.

_____ I have positioned my subpoints under the main points to which they are related.

_____ My conclusion contains a summary that recaps my message and remarks that reflect on the meaning and significance of my speech.

_____ I have provided transitions where they are needed to make my speech flow smoothly.

_____ I have compiled a list of the works that I consulted in the preparation of my speech.

Copyright © Houghton Mifflin Company. All rights reserved.

Guidelines for Using a Sequential Design

A sequential design may be used to present the steps of a process or to provide a historical perspective on a subject.

When using a sequential design to present the steps in a process, you must first determine the necessary steps and the order in which they must take place. These steps will become the main points of the speech. For an oral presentation, you should not try to discuss more than five steps. If you have more than five, see if you can cluster some of them into subpoints. Be sure to enumerate the steps as you present them so that the audience can follow your message.

When using a sequential design to present a historical perspective on a subject, be sure to follow a systematic chronological sequence. Do not jump around in time (i.e., don't start with 1990, jump back to 1942, and then fast forward to 1971) or the speech will be difficult for your listeners to follow. You can either start with the beginnings of a subject and trace it to a later point in time or begin with the present and trace the subject back to its origins. When presenting a historical perspective, it is important to narrow your topic to manageable proportions by selecting the most important historical occurrences. Your speech should telescope time.

Copyright © Houghton Mifflin Company. All rights reserved.

Outline Worksheet: Sequential Design

Title (optional): _____

Topic: _____

Specific purpose: _____

_____

Thesis statement: _____

_____

Introduction

Attention material: _____

_____

Credibility material: _____

_____

Preview: _____

_____

(Transition to body of speech)

_____

Body

I. Main point #1 (Step or Occurrence 1): _____

_____

    A. (subpoint): _____

_____

    B. (subpoint): _____

_____

(Transition to Main point #2)

_____

Copyright © Houghton Mifflin Company. All rights reserved.

II. Main point #2 (Step or Occurrence 2): _____

_____

    A. (subpoint): _____

    _____

    B. (subpoint): _____

    _____

(Transition to Main point #3)

_____

III. Main point #3 (Step or Occurrence 3): _____

_____

    A. (subpoint): _____

    _____

    B. (subpoint): _____

    _____

(Transition to Main point #4)

_____

IV. Main point #4 (Step or Occurrence 4): _____

_____

    A. (subpoint): _____

    _____

    B. (subpoint): _____

    _____

(Transition to Main point #5)

_____

Copyright © Houghton Mifflin Company. All rights reserved.

V. Main point #5 (Step or Occurrence 5): _____

_____

    A. (subpoint): _____

    _____

    B. (subpoint): _____

    _____

(Transition to conclusion)

_____

Conclusion

    Summary: _____

    _____

    Concluding remarks: _____

    _____

Works Consulted:

Copyright © Houghton Mifflin Company. All rights reserved.

Checklist for a Sequential Design

_____ My topic involves a process that can be explained as a series of steps or a subject on which I wish to provide a historical perspective.

_____ I have clearly stated the purpose of my speech.

_____ My thesis statement is written as a complete declarative sentence.

_____ My introduction gains attention and interest, establishes my credibility, and previews the main points of my message.

_____ I have determined the main steps that must be taken (if applicable).

_____ I have arranged the steps in the order in which they must be taken (if applicable).

_____ I have selected the major occurrences or developments related to my topic (if applicable).

_____ I have presented the occurrences chronologically (if applicable).

_____ I have adequate supporting material for each main point in my speech.

_____ I have positioned my subpoints under the main points to which they are related.

_____ My conclusion contains a summary that recaps my message and remarks that reflect on the meaning and significance of my speech.

_____ I have provided transitions where they are needed to make my speech flow smoothly.

_____ I have compiled a list of the works that I consulted in the preparation of my speech.

Copyright © Houghton Mifflin Company. All rights reserved.

Guidelines for Using a Categorical Design

You should use a categorical design for subjects that have natural or customary divisions. This design allows you to organize large amounts of material into a manageable format. Do not use a categorical design by default—i.e., because you are too lazy to think of any other way to arrange your information.

When you are using a categorical design, each category becomes a main point for the development of your speech. Limit yourself to five or fewer main points in a short speech. You should begin and end with the most important categories since the first and last areas covered are the most easily remembered.

Copyright © Houghton Mifflin Company. All rights reserved.

Outline Worksheet: Categorical Design

Title (optional): _____

Topic: _____

Specific purpose: _____

_____

Thesis statement: _____

_____

Introduction

Attention material: _____

_____

Credibility material: _____

_____

Preview: _____

_____

(Transition to body of speech)

_____

Body

I. Main point #1 (first category): _____

_____

    A. (subpoint): _____

_____

    B. (subpoint): _____

_____

(Transition to Main point #2)

_____

Copyright © Houghton Mifflin Company. All rights reserved.

II. Main point #2 (second category): _____

_____

    A. (subpoint): _____

_____

    B. (subpoint): _____

_____

(Transition to Main point #3)

_____

III. Main point #3 (third category): _____

_____

    A. (subpoint): _____

_____

    B. (subpoint): _____

_____

(Transition to Main point #4)

_____

IV. Main point #4 (fourth category): _____

_____

    A. (subpoint): _____

_____

    B. (subpoint): _____

_____

(Transition to Main point #5)

_____

Copyright © Houghton Mifflin Company. All rights reserved.

V. Main point #5 (fifth category): _____

_____

    A. (subpoint): _____

    _____

    B. (subpoint): _____

    _____

(Transition to conclusion)

_____

Conclusion

    Summary: _____

    _____

    Concluding remarks: _____

    _____

Works Consulted:

Copyright © Houghton Mifflin Company. All rights reserved.

Checklist for a Categorical Design

_____ I have selected a topic that has natural or customary divisions.

_____ I have clearly stated the purpose of my speech.

_____ My thesis statement is written as a complete declarative sentence.

_____ My introduction gains attention and interest, establishes my credibility, and previews the main points of my message.

_____ I have no more than five categories as main points in my speech.

_____ I have arranged my speech so that the most important categories are presented first and last.

_____ I have positioned my subpoints under the main points to which they are related.

_____ My conclusion contains a summary that recaps my message and remarks that reflect on the meaning and significance of the speech.

_____ I have provided transitions where they are needed to make my speech flow smoothly.

_____ I have compiled a list of the works that I consulted in the preparation of my speech.

Copyright © Houghton Mifflin Company. All rights reserved.

Guidelines for Using a Comparative Design

You may wish to use a comparative design if your topic is new to your audience, abstract, highly technical, or simply difficult to understand. The comparative design aids understanding by relating your topic to something the audience already knows and comprehends. It may take the form of a literal analogy, a figurative analogy, or a comparison and contrast showing both similarities and differences.

The body of a speech using a comparative design may include up to five main similarities or differences. In a literal analogy, the topics are drawn from the same area. For example, word processing and typing are two ways to produce written information by using a keyboard, so the comparison between them is literal. In a figurative analogy, the speaker draws together topics from different areas. For example, you could relate the body's struggle against infection to a military campaign by identifying who or what makes up the armies, how they fight, and the consequences of victory or defeat. In a comparison and contrast design, you show how two things are both similar and different.

Copyright © Houghton Mifflin Company. All rights reserved.

Outline Worksheet: Comparative Design

Title (optional): _____

Topic: _____

Specific purpose: _____

_____

Thesis statement: _____

_____

Introduction

Attention material: _____

_____

Credibility material: _____

_____

Preview: _____

_____

(Transition to body of speech)

_____

Body

I. Main point #1 (first similarity or difference): _____

_____

    A. (subpoint): _____

_____

    B. (subpoint): _____

_____

(Transition to Main point #2)

_____

Copyright © Houghton Mifflin Company. All rights reserved.

II. Main point #2 (second similarity or difference): _____

_____

    A. (subpoint): _____

    _____

    B. (subpoint): _____

    _____

(Transition to Main point #3)

_____

III. Main point #3 (third similarity or difference): _____

_____

    A. (subpoint): _____

    _____

    B. (subpoint): _____

    _____

(Transition to Main point #4)

_____

IV. Main point #4 (fourth similarity or difference): _____

_____

    A. (subpoint): _____

    _____

    B. (subpoint): _____

    _____

(Transition to Main point #5)

_____

Copyright © Houghton Mifflin Company. All rights reserved.

V. Main point #5 (fifth similarity or difference): _____

_____

    A. (subpoint): _____

    _____

    B. (subpoint): _____

    _____

(Transition to conclusion)

_____

Conclusion

    Summary: _____

    _____

    Concluding remarks: _____

    _____

Works Consulted:

Copyright © Houghton Mifflin Company. All rights reserved.

Checklist for a Comparative Design

_____ I have selected a topic that is unfamiliar, abstract, or otherwise difficult to understand.

_____ The purpose of my speech is to compare and/or contrast two or more similar or dissimilar objects, ideas, situations, people, or events.

_____ I have clearly stated the purpose of my speech.

_____ My thesis statement is written as a complete declarative sentence.

_____ My introduction gains attention and interest, establishes my credibility, and previews the main points of my message.

_____ Each of my main points addresses one point of comparison or contrast.

_____ Each of my main points is supported with facts, statistics, testimony, examples, or narratives.

_____ The comparisons or contrasts I make are not strained.

_____ I have positioned subpoints under the main points to which they are related.

_____ I have included a summary statement that reviews the comparisons and contrasts.

_____ I have prepared concluding remarks that reflect on the meaning and significance of my message.

_____ I have provided transitions where they are needed to make my speech flow smoothly.

_____ I have compiled a list of the works that I consulted in the preparation of my speech.

Copyright © Houghton Mifflin Company. All rights reserved.

Guidelines for Using a Causation Design

You may wish to use a causation design for a speech of explanation that tries to make the world and the things in it more understandable. The causation design explains a situation, condition, or event in terms of the causes that led up to it.

The body of a causation design typically begins with a description of existing conditions, then probes for its causes. The description of existing conditions becomes the first main point in the speech, with the causes being subsequent main points.

The causes may be separated into categories, which can then be arranged in order of their importance. The causes may also be presented in a historical design, which may begin with the distant past and work up to the present, begin with the present and work back to the origin of the situation, or begin with the present and make projections into the future.

Copyright © Houghton Mifflin Company. All rights reserved.

Outline Worksheet: Causation Design

Title (optional): _____

Topic: _____

Specific purpose: _____

_____

Thesis statement: _____

_____

Introduction

Attention material: _____

_____

Credibility material: _____

_____

Preview: _____

_____

(Transition to body of speech)

_____

Body

I. Main point #1 (description of existing conditions): _____

_____

    A. (subpoint): _____

_____

    B. (subpoint): _____

_____

(Transition to Main point #2)

_____

Copyright © Houghton Mifflin Company. All rights reserved.

II. Main point #2 (first cause): _____

_____

    A. (subpoint): _____

    _____

    B. (subpoint): _____

    _____

(Transition to Main point #3)

_____

III. Main point #3 (second cause): _____

_____

    A. (subpoint): _____

    _____

    B. (subpoint): _____

    _____

(Transition to Main point #4)

_____

IV. Main point #4 (third cause): _____

_____

    A. (subpoint): _____

    _____

    B. (subpoint): _____

    _____

(Transition to Main point #5)

_____

Copyright © Houghton Mifflin Company. All rights reserved.

V. Main point #5 (fourth cause): _____

_____

    A. (subpoint): _____

_____

    B. (subpoint): _____

_____

(Transition to conclusion)

_____

Conclusion

    Summary: _____

_____

    Concluding remarks: _____

_____

Works Consulted:

Copyright © Houghton Mifflin Company. All rights reserved.

Checklist for a Causation Design

_____ I have selected a topic that involves a situation, condition, or event that can best be understood in terms of its causes.

_____ I have clearly stated the purpose of my speech.

_____ My thesis statement is written as a complete declarative sentence.

_____ My introduction gains attention and interest, establishes my credibility, and previews the main points of my message.

_____ The first main point of my speech describes the present condition, situation, or event.

_____ The subsequent main points of my speech explain the causes of the condition, situation, or event.

_____ The main points containing causes are arranged either categorically in terms of their importance or chronologically (see categorical and sequential designs).

_____ I have been careful not to oversimplify the cause-effect relationships.

_____ I have positioned my subpoints under the main points to which they are related.

_____ My conclusion contains a summary that recaps my message and remarks that reflect on the meaning and significance of my speech.

_____ I have provided transitions where they are needed to make my speech flow smoothly.

_____ I have compiled a list of the works that I consulted in the preparation of my speech.

Copyright © Houghton Mifflin Company. All rights reserved.

Guidelines for Using a Problem-Solution Design

You may wish to use a problem-solution design when you must convince your audience that they should face up to a specific problem and that you have a solution that will deal with it. It is sometimes difficult to convince people that there really is a problem that deserves or possibly even demands their attention. People often ignore problems until they reach a critical stage when drastic action is necessary. You can counteract this attitude by depicting the crisis that will arise unless the audience makes the changes that you suggest. The solution phase of a problem-solution design typically involves changing an attitude or taking action.

The body of a problem-solution design usually has only two main points: the presentation of the problem and the presentation of the solution. Subpoints under the problem main point describe the problem, highlight its importance, and suggest what might happen if the problem is ignored. Subpoints under the solution main point describe the solution, show how it solves the problem, present a plan of action, and picture the results of its implementation.

Copyright © Houghton Mifflin Company. All rights reserved.

Outline Worksheet: Problem-Solution Design

Title (optional): _____

Topic: _____

Specific purpose: _____

_____

Thesis statement: _____

_____

Introduction

Attention material: _____

_____

Credibility material: _____

_____

Preview: _____

_____

(Transition to body of speech)

_____

Body

I. Main point #1 (Statement of problem): _____

_____

    A. (Description of problem): _____

_____

        1. (Signs, symptoms, effects of problem): _____

_____

        2. (Example, narrative, or testimony): _____

_____

Copyright © Houghton Mifflin Company. All rights reserved.

B. (Importance of problem): _____

_____

    1. (Extent of problem): _____

_____

        a. (Facts/statistics): _____

_____

        b. (Expert testimony): _____

_____

    2. (Who is affected?): _____

_____

        a. (Facts/statistics): _____

_____

        b. (Example/narrative): _____

_____

C. (Consequences of problem): _____

_____

    1. (Expert testimony): _____

_____

    2. (Example/narrative): _____

_____

(Transition to Main point #2)

_____

II. Main point #2 (Statement of solution): _____

_____

    A. (Description of solution): _____

_____

Copyright © Houghton Mifflin Company. All rights reserved.

1. (How solution fits problem): _____

_____

   a. (More than symptom relief): _____

   _____

   b. (Is workable): _____

   _____

2. (How solution can be implemented): _____

_____

   a. (Plan of action): _____

   _____

      (1) (Step #1 of plan): _____

      _____

      (2) (Step #2 of plan): _____

      _____

      (3) (Step #3 of plan): _____

      _____

      (4) (Step #4 of plan): _____

      _____

   b. (Costs and efforts): _____

   _____

B. (Picture results): _____

_____

   1. (Describe expected results): _____

   _____

   2. (When results expected): _____

   _____

   3. (Additional benefits): _____

   _____

Copyright © Houghton Mifflin Company. All rights reserved.

(Transition to conclusion)

_____

Conclusion

Summary: _____

_____

Concluding remarks: _____

_____

Works Consulted:

Copyright © Houghton Mifflin Company. All rights reserved.

Checklist for a Problem-Solution Design

_____ I have selected a topic that involves a problem that needs to be solved.

_____ I have clearly stated the purpose of my speech.

_____ My thesis statement is written as a complete declarative sentence.

_____ My introduction gains attention and interest, establishes my credibility, and previews the main points of my message.

_____ My first main point presents the problem.

_____ My subpoints for the first main point describe the problem, show its importance, and demonstrate the consequences of inaction.

_____ I have adequate supporting material for each of my subpoints relating to the problem.

_____ My second main point presents my solution to the problem.

_____ My subpoints for the second main point demonstrate how the solution addresses the problem, describes a plan of action, and pictures the results of the solution.

_____ I have adequate supporting material for each of my subpoints relating to the solution.

_____ My conclusion contains a summary that recaps my message and remarks that reflect on the meaning and significance of my speech.

_____ I have provided transitions where they are needed to make my speech flow smoothly.

_____ I have compiled a list of the works that I consulted in the preparation of my speech.

Copyright © Houghton Mifflin Company. All rights reserved.

Guidelines for Using a Motivated Sequence Design

You may wish to use a motivated sequence design for a persuasive speech intended to move people to action. The motivated sequence design is a highly structured variation of the problem-solution design. It concentrates on awakening an awareness of a need and then shows how that need can be satisfied, concluding with an explicit call for action. The motivated sequence contains five steps: 1) focusing attention on a problem, 2) demonstrating a need, 3) presenting a solution to satisfy that need, 4) visualizing the results of the implementation of the solution, and 4) issuing a call for action.

The first step in the motivated sequence design comes in the introduction of the speech. In the motivated sequence design, the introduction should arouse attention and directly focus this attention on the problem that will be addressed in the speech.

The second through fourth steps in the motivated sequence design are covered in the body of the speech, which will typically contain three main points. The first main point of the body of the speech covers Step 2 of the motivated sequence design. It should be used to demonstrate a need related to the problem. The second main point of the body of the speech covers Step 3 of the motivated sequence design. It should present a detailed plan of action to satisfy the need. The third main point of the body of the speech covers Step 4 of the motivated sequence design. It should picture the positive results that will occur if the plan is adopted and/or the negative results that might be expected if the plan is ignored.

The fifth step in the motivated sequence design comes in the conclusion of the speech. It is a call for action.

When you are using the motivated sequence design, audience analysis is extremely important, For example, if the audience already recognizes that there is a need for action, that step in the sequence can be covered briefly, and the major thrust of the speech would address the plan, visualization of results, and the call for action. Similarly, if the audience is convinced of the need and is familiar with the plan but needs its momentum renewed or needs to be prodded into action, the focus of the speech would be on visualizing the results and calling for action.

Copyright © Houghton Mifflin Company. All rights reserved.

Outline Worksheet: Motivated Sequence Design

Title (optional): _____

Topic: _____

Specific purpose: _____

_____

Thesis statement: _____

_____

Introduction

Attention material (focus attention on problem): _____

_____

Credibility material: _____

_____

Preview: _____

_____

(Transition to body of speech)

_____

Body

I. Main point #1 (Statement of need for action): _____

_____

    A. (Description of problem): _____

_____

        1. (Signs, symptoms, effects of problem): _____

_____

        2. (Example, narrative, or testimony): _____

_____

Copyright © Houghton Mifflin Company. All rights reserved.

B. (Importance of problem): _____

_____

    1. (Extent of problem): _____

    _____

        a. (Facts/statistics): _____

        _____

        b. (Expert testimony): _____

        _____

    2. (Who is affected?): _____

    _____

        a. (Facts/statistics): _____

        _____

        b. (Example/narrative): _____

        _____

(Transition to Main point #2)

_____

II. Main point #2 (Present solution that satisfies need): _____

_____

    A. (Description of solution): _____

    _____

        1. (How solution satisfies need): _____

        _____

        2. (How solution can be implemented): _____

        _____

            a. (Plan of action): _____

            _____

Copyright © Houghton Mifflin Company. All rights reserved.

(1) (Step #1 of plan): _____

_____

(2) (Step #2 of plan): _____

_____

(3) (Step #3 of plan): _____

_____

(4) (Step #4 of plan): _____

_____

(Transition to Main point #3)

_____

III. (Visualize results): _____

_____

    1. (Describe expected results of action): _____

_____

    2. (Describe consequences of inaction): _____

_____

(Transition to conclusion)

_____

Conclusion

Summary: _____

_____

Call for action: _____

_____

Works Consulted:

Copyright © Houghton Mifflin Company. All rights reserved.

Checklist for a Motivated Sequence Design

_____ I have selected a topic that involves a problem that needs to be solved with action.

_____ I have clearly stated the purpose of my speech.

_____ My thesis statement is written as a complete declarative sentence.

_____ My introduction focuses attention on the problem, establishes my credibility, and previews my message.

_____ The first main point in my speech establishes the need for action.

_____ The second main point in my speech details a plan of action that satisfies the need.

_____ The third main point in my speech visualizes the results of action and the consequences of inaction.

_____ I have appropriate supporting material for each main point in my speech.

_____ The conclusion of my speech contains a summary statement and ends with a call for action.

_____ I have provided transitions where they are needed to make my speech flow smoothly.

_____ I have compiled a list of the works that I consulted in the preparation of my speech.

Copyright © Houghton Mifflin Company. All rights reserved.

Guidelines for Using a Refutative Design

You may wish to use a refutative design to raise doubts about, damage, or even destroy an opposing position by pointing out its weaknesses and inconsistencies. To make an effective refutation, you must be thoroughly familiar with the points that the opposition would make in an argument. It is wise to attack the weakest points or arguments first. Don't try to refute more than three points or arguments in a short classroom presentation. Base your refutations on faulty reasoning or inadequate evidence. Avoid personal attacks on opponents unless credibility issues are inescapable. If time permits, support an alternative point or argument to replace the one(s) you have refuted.

In the body of your speech, your main points will be the points or arguments that you are refuting or supporting. Refutation follows a five-step sequence: 1) state the point you will refute and explain its importance to the opposing position, 2) tell how you will refute the point, 3) present evidence to refute the point, 4) show how the evidence refutes the point, and 5) explain the significance of the refutation. A refutative speech is strengthened if you can support an alternative point or argument for each one that you refute. Use the same five steps to demonstrate the superiority of your position. The inclusion of a supported point helps to counteract the negativity associated with straight refutation and provides the audience with a sense of completeness and closure.

Copyright © Houghton Mifflin Company. All rights reserved.

Outline Worksheet: Refutative Design

Title (optional): _____

Topic: _____

Specific purpose: _____

_____

Thesis statement: _____

_____

Introduction

Attention material: _____

_____

Credibility material: _____

_____

Preview: _____

_____

(Transition to body of speech)

_____

Body

I. Main point #1 (first point you will refute/weakest point of opposition): _____

_____

    A. (Explain importance of point): _____

_____

    B. (Explain how you will refute point): _____

_____

    C. (Present evidence to refute point): _____

_____

Copyright © Houghton Mifflin Company. All rights reserved.

1. (Facts/figures): _____

_____

2. (Expert testimony): _____

_____

D. (Explain how evidence refutes point): _____

_____

E. (Explain significance of refutation): _____

_____

    1. (Facts/figures/expert testimony): _____

    _____

    2. (Example/narrative): _____

    _____

(Transition to Main point #2)

_____

II. Main point #2 (second point you will refute or counterpoint you will support): _____

_____

A. (Explain importance of point): _____

_____

B. (Explain how you will refute/support point): _____

_____

C. (Present evidence to refute/support point): _____

_____

    1. (Facts/figures): _____

    _____

    2. (Expert testimony): _____

    _____

Copyright © Houghton Mifflin Company. All rights reserved.

D. (Explain how evidence refutes/supports point): _____

_____

E. (Explain significance of refutation/support): _____

_____

    1. (Facts/figures/expert testimony): _____

    _____

    2. (Example/narrative): _____

    _____

(Transition to Main point #3)

_____

III. Main point #3 (second/third point you will refute): _____

_____

A. (Explain importance of point): _____

_____

B. (Explain how you will refute point): _____

_____

C. (Present evidence to refute point): _____

_____

    1. (Facts/figures): _____

    _____

    2. (Expert testimony): _____

    _____

D. (Explain how evidence refutes point): _____

_____

E. (Explain significance of refutation): _____

_____

Copyright © Houghton Mifflin Company. All rights reserved.

1. (Facts/figures/expert testimony): _____

_____

2. (Example/narrative): _____

_____

(Transition to Main point #4)

_____

IV. Main point #4 (next point you will refute or counterpoint you will support): _____

_____

   A. (Explain importance of point): _____

_____

   B. (Explain how you will refute/support point): _____

_____

   C. (Present evidence to refute/support point): _____

_____

      1. (Facts/figures): _____

_____

      2. (Expert testimony): _____

_____

   D. (Explain how evidence refutes/supports point): _____

_____

   E. (Explain significance of refutation/support): _____

_____

      1. (Facts/figures/expert testimony): _____

_____

      2. (Example/narrative): _____

_____

Copyright © Houghton Mifflin Company. All rights reserved.

(Transition to conclusion)

Conclusion

Summary: _____

_____

Concluding remarks: _____

_____

Works Consulted:

Copyright © Houghton Mifflin Company. All rights reserved.

Checklist for a Refutative Design

_____ I have selected a topic that involves an issue that has strong opposition.

_____ I have clearly stated the purpose of my speech.

_____ My thesis statement is written as a complete declarative sentence.

_____ My introduction gains attention and interest, establishes my credibility, and previews the main points of my message.

_____ My first main point refutes the opposition's weakest point.

_____ Each main point for refutation is clearly stated, and its importance is explained.

_____ I describe how I will attack each point and present credible evidence to support my refutation.

_____ I clearly explain what each refutation means.

_____ I have supported a counterpoint for each point that I have refuted, following the same format used for each refutation.

_____ I have avoided personal attacks in my refutations.

_____ My conclusion contains a summary that recaps my message and concluding remarks that reflect on the meaning and significance of my speech.

_____ I have provided transitions where they are needed to make my speech flow smoothly.

_____ I have compiled a list of the works that I consulted in preparation for my speech.

Copyright © Houghton Mifflin Company. All rights reserved.

DATE DUE